FILM FOCUS

Ronald Gottesman and Harry M. Geduld
General Editors

The Film Focus series presents the best that has been written about the art of film and the men who created it. Combining criticism with history, biography, and analysis of technique, the volumes in the series explore the many dimensions of the film medium and its impact on modern society.

Birgitta Steene, *editor of this volume in the Film Focus series, is Associate Professor of English at Temple University. She has lectured widely on the contemporary Swedish film and has written books on Ingmar Bergman and August Strindberg, as well as numerous articles on modern drama and film.*

FOCUS ON

THE SEVENTH SEAL

edited by

BIRGITTA STEENE

A SPECTRUM BOOK

Prentice-Hall, Inc.
Englewood Cliffs, N.J.

Library of Congress Cataloging in Publication Data

Steene, Birgitta, comp.
  Focus on The seventh seal.

  (Film Focus)
  (A spectrum book)
  Bibliography: p.
  1. Bergman, Ingmar, 1918–   Det Sjunde inseglet.
I. Title.
PN1997.B3943S8   791.43'7   76–178766
ISBN   0–13–806927–1
ISBN   0–13–806919–0 (pbk.)

For Mika,
my young film buff

Illustrations from *The Seventh Seal*
are reprinted by permission
of AB Svensk Filmindustri.

© 1972 by PRENTICE-HALL, INC.
Englewood Cliffs, New Jersey

A SPECTRUM BOOK

10   9   8   7   6   5   4   3   2   1

PRENTICE-HALL INTERNATIONAL, INC. (*London*)
PRENTICE-HALL OF AUSTRALIA, PTY. LTD. (*Sydney*)
PRENTICE-HALL OF CANADA, LTD. (*Toronto*)
PRENTICE-HALL OF INDIA PRIVATE LIMITED (*New Delhi*)
PRENTICE-HALL OF JAPAN, INC. (*Tokyo*)

CONTENTS

v

ESSAYS

COMMENTARIES

PREFACE

I want to thank the following libraries for assisting me in obtaining material for this volume:

The Swedish Film Institute
The Royal Library, Stockholm
Bibliotekstjänst, Lund
The British Film Institute
The Royal Library, Edinburgh
The British Museum
Cine Club del Uruguay
Hochschule für Fernsehen und Film, Munich
The Lincoln branch of the New York Public Library
The UCLA Library

My special thanks to Monica Letzring of Temple University for checking the manuscript for me, and to Janus Films, Inc., for arranging for a complimentary showing of *The Seventh Seal.*

THE SEVENTH SEAL

(*Det sjunde inseglet*)

AB Svensk Filmindustri, 1956. Producer: Allan Ekelund

SCREENPLAY	Ingmar Bergman
DIRECTION	Ingmar Bergman
ASSISTANT DIRECTOR	Lennart Ohlsson
PHOTOGRAPHY	Gunnar Fischer
EDITING	Lennart Wallén
CHOREOGRAPHY	Else Fischer
DECORS	P-A. Lundgren
MUSIC	Erik Nordgren

TIME: 96 MINUTES

Filmed in the summer of 1956 at Hovs Hallar, Sweden, and Svensk Filmindustri's studios at Råsunda, Stockholm. Premiere: February 16, 1957, Röda Kvarn, Stockholm.

CAST

The Knight	MAX VON SYDOW
The Squire	GUNNAR BJÖRNSTRAND
Death	BENGT EKEROT
Jof	NILS POPPE
Mia	BIBI ANDERSSON
Plog, the Smith	ÅKE FRIDELL
Lisa, Plog's wife	INGA GILL
Skat	ERIK STRANDMARK
The Witch	MAUD HANSSON
The Mute Girl	GUNNEL LINDBLOM
Raval	BERTIL ANDERBERG
The Monk	ANDERS EK
The Church Painter	GUNNAR OLSSON
The Merchant	BENGT-ÅKE BENKTSSON
The Woman in the Tavern	GUDRUN BROST
The Leader of the Soldiers	ULF JOHANSSON
The Young Monk	LARS LIND
The Knight's Wife	INGA LANDGRÉ

Introduction

THE SEVENTH SEAL:
Film as Doomsday Metaphor
by BIRGITTA STEENE

The year 1956 was a good year for Ingmar Bergman. In May his film *Smiles of a Summer Night* won international recognition at the Cannes festival. His time of apprenticeship and struggle seemed over and now he could finally proceed to make the film that had been on his mind for a long time: *The Seventh Seal*. In the hectic mood of the festival he met and talked about his next project with his producer Carl Anders Dymling. Years later Dr. Dymling reminisced about the occasion:

> As a producer I was quite aware of the financial risk in a motion picture with so serious a theme. But it promised to be an unusual, an outstanding picture. It *had* to be done. We discussed the script for several days and nights during the Cannes festival in May 1956. We agreed on some changes, on the cast and on the budget. We felt as if we were launching a big ship and we were very happy.[1]

We have no reason to doubt Dr. Dymling's statement; yet it does not tell very much about the rather involved history of *The Seventh Seal* from original idea to actual film project. To a certain extent it is a history that should be related to the difficult years in the early 1950s when the Swedish film industry catered almost exclusively

[1] From "A Preface," in *Four Screenplays of Ingmar Bergman* (New York: Simon & Schuster, Inc., 1960), p. x.

to an unsophisticated national market and was in deep financial
trouble because of high revenues. A strike paralyzed Swedish filmmaking in 1950. (Bergman spent the time making soap commercials.
In one of them a swineherd is kissed by a young princess, who
happens to be fifteen-year-old Bibi Andersson. Six years later she
was to play the role of young Mia in *The Seventh Seal* and she has
remained Bergman's most faithful actress.)

When a settlement was reached and the strike called off, the
budgetary strings were tightened and Bergman's artistic intentions
were somewhat stymied. One of his most interesting early films, *The
Naked Night* (lit. *The Eve of Clowns*), was rejected by his company,
Svensk Filmindustri, in spite of the fact that his three preceding
films (*Illicit Interlude, Secrets of Women,* and *Summer with Monica*)
had made a modest profit at the box office. Bergman found a producer elsewhere (Rune Waldecrantz at Sandrews), but though *The
Naked Night* was awarded a prize at a São Paulo (Brazil) film festival in 1954, the public at home did not respond well to it. One
Stockholm paper (*Aftonbladet,* September 15, 1953) referred to it
simply as "Bergman's latest vomit."

Somewhat later, when Bergman—now reconciled with Svensk
Filmindustri—suggested that he make a film based on a play script
of his own about a medieval knight torn by metaphysical *Angst,*
his producer flatly refused it. In order to survive, his company
needed films that would draw crowds. Bergman went ahead and
published his play, called *Wood Painting,*[2] which he had used
earlier as a pedagogical exercise for his actors at the Malmö City
Theater where he was stage director in the early fifties.

Wood Painting reached the prestigious Royal Dramatic Stage in
Stockholm a year later (1955),[3] but Bergman was not able to con-
vince Svensk Filmindustri of its cinematic potential. He had in fact
begun to have serious doubts about his future as a filmmaker and
for a while had plunged into a deep depression. But like Chekhov,
who once claimed that he wrote tragic dramas when he was happy
and comedies when he felt miserable, Bergman too turned to the

---

[2] Trämålning. In *Svenska Radiopjäser 1954,* Stockholm: Radiotjänst, 1954.
Reprinted in this volume, pp. 159–73.
[3] The Stockholm production of *Wood Painting* was directed by Bengt Ekerot,
who later played Death in *The Seventh Seal.* Bibi Andersson—Mia in the film—
played the role of Lisa, the Smith's wife. The rest of the cast for *The Seventh
Seal* Bergman recruited among actors he had met at the Malmö City Theater.

comic mode during his despondency. Seizing upon the favorable response to the comic elevator episode in his 1952 film *Secrets of Women,* Bergman wrote and directed a full-length erotic comedy, *A Lesson in Love,* casting it with the same actors (Eva Dahlbeck and Gunnar Björnstrand). The film became a popular success within Sweden and with renewed hope Bergman returned to his producers: Would they now perhaps consider his script about the medieval knight?

But again Bergman was told to forget about his brooding Crusader and was advised to think seriously about making another erotic comedy. A year later he had finished *Smiles of a Summer Night.*

The film was sent to Cannes almost by accident and the critical acclaim it won at the festival took Swedish producers and critics by surprise. As a matter of fact, about the same time as Bergman's film was praised by film people at Cannes, a scathing parody of it by comedian Povel Ramel was shown throughout Sweden. The old adage that no one is a prophet in his own country has often held true for Ingmar Bergman.

Bergman himself was rather startled by the success of his film at Cannes. But he realized that now was his chance to persuade a producer to let him film *The Seventh Seal.* In a recent interview Bergman has given us an amusing account of the entire episode:

> I was out in the privvy reading the newspaper. Suddenly I read: "Swedish Film Wins Prize at Cannes," "Swedish Film a Sensation at Cannes" or something like that. What the devil, I thought, which film can that be? I didn't believe my eyes when I saw that they meant *Smiles of a Summer Night.*
>
> Then I travelled down to see Carl Anders Dymling with the script to *The Seventh Seal,* for the producers at Sandrews had alluded to the fact that they were still counting the losses from *Waiting Women* and *The Naked Night,* so they weren't interested. So then I went down to Carl Anders with the script for *The Seventh Seal* and put it on his desk—he was on the phone selling *Smiles of a Summer Night* to all sorts of countries. He was in a boisterous mood; he was sitting on Oriental rugs looking at Picasso and was happy about everything. So I said: "Now, Carl Anders, now or never!" And then I put *The Seventh Seal* right in front of him and said: "Now, make up your mind!" [4]

[4] Stig Björkman, Torsten Manns and Jonas Sima. *Bergman om Bergman.* Stockholm: P. A. Norstedt & Söners Förlag, 1970, p. 109.

And that is when and how Dr. Dymling came to decide to encourage his young protégé to make *The Seventh Seal*.

At Hovs Hallar in southern Sweden, Bergman had long since found the landscape he wanted for the setting of the film: wild bluffs overlooking a wide expanse of grey ocean, with moors stretching inland to a forest that seemed inhabited by trolls and other creatures of the folk imagination. Ironically enough, however, only the beach and plateau scenes were actually filmed on location. The rest of the film was shot just outside of Stockholm and in Svensk Filmindustri's outdoor and indoor studios. The shooting of the entire ninety-six-minute film was done in 35 days. It turned out to be one of the most economical feature-length films of all times: the total cost did not much exceed $125,000, which is truly remarkable when one considers the film's painstaking reproduction of the medieval milieu and costumes, as well as its elements of epic spectacle in, for instance, the flagellant sequence.

To many viewers of Bergman films, *The Seventh Seal* remains a favorite. As Bosley Crowther, whose essay on the film is included in this volume, has said, *The Seventh Seal* belongs to those crucial pictures that have opened up new cinematic ground both technically and thematically. Here is indeed a film that has become a modern classic, that is, a work to which we go back not only for its film historical importance but, even more, for its rather unique capacity to evoke in us some of the original excitement we felt when viewing it for the first time back in 1957. Its visual splendor has not faded even if its philosophical theme has tended to become overexposed by content-oriented critics.

The Seventh Seal, which won the jury's special prize at the 1957 Cannes film festival, arrived upon the international scene at an opportune moment. At least part of the film's success outside of Sweden can be related to a cultural vogue. The metaphysical malaise of the 1950s, transferred from the earlier novels of Kafka to the nonaction plays of Samuel Beckett, had created a climate that was ripe for a film like *The Seventh Seal*, with its portrait of *Angst*-ridden, existentialist man posing the eternal questions about the meaning of life and the horror of death and total annihilation.

The growing reality of the hydrogen bomb, now stored in enough quantities to obliterate the human race from the face of the earth, created a doomsday atmosphere among many artists and intellectuals in Europe, who had no difficulty following Bergman when he suggested an analogy between the plague-ridden fourteenth-century world of his film and the modern atomic age: "In my film the Crusader returns from the Crusades as the soldier returns from the war today. In the Middle Ages man lived in terror of the plague. Today they live in fear of the atomic bomb." [5] To this, one might add that the movie-going public of our apocalyptic 1970s, for whom thoughts of ecological disasters have in part replaced fears of atomic destruction, can still experience *The Seventh Seal* as a meaningful doomsday metaphor.

The Seventh Seal has had its firmest supporters in France and the United States. In reading reviews and articles on the film in such magazines as *Cahiers du Cinéma, Image et Son, Télé-Ciné, Film Culture,* and *Film Quarterly*—magazines with a somewhat academic orientation—one is immediately struck by a tendency among the critics to emphasize *The Seventh Seal* as a philosophical credo on the screen, the work of a filmmaker with a personal vision.[6] With *The Seventh Seal* Bergman became the protégé of *cinéastes* in Paris, who treated him as a prototypal *auteur du cinéma*. It is not surprising to find that in the United States Bergman's film was most profoundly analyzed by a firm supporter of *Cahiers du Cinéma,* critic Andrew Sarris of the *Village Voice*. To this day Andrew Sarris' essay on *The Seventh Seal,* first printed in *Film Culture,* is one of the most balanced and exhaustive analyses of the film.

In recent years Bergman's films have become the subject of several doctoral dissertations and book-length studies, especially in the United States. Most of these works are written by people in noncinematic fields, such as literature, philosophy, or religion. Publishers sometimes seem to assume that such humanist-oriented film analyses can be meaningful even to readers without a firsthand knowledge of the film. For example, a book by theology professor Arthur Gibson, entitled *The Silence of God,* appeared with the following blurb on its dust jacket: "Readers who haven't seen Bergman's pictures may be helped by Gibson's synopsis of each." To counteract such a view, I have purposely tried to avoid too much material which treats the film *exclusively* as message.

The critic who is inclined toward theme and content can of course have a field day with *The Seventh Seal,* as with all of Berg-

---

[5] From a program note issued by Svensk Filmindustri, Stockholm, 1957.

[6] German, Italian, and Latin American critics have also been inclined to stress the *philosophical* theme of *The Seventh Seal.*

man's published screenplays, which read like literary works rather than shooting scripts.[7] Besides, *The Seventh Seal* invites one to make comparisons with earlier literary genres. It shares an allegorical framework, for example, with the medieval morality play, but Bergman's method, as a great many critics have pointed out, is suggestive rather than precisely conceptualized and altogether coherent. For this reason some reviewers, among them Henry Hart, have accused Bergman of being a nasty cinematic Bluebeard hoarding the answers to his enigmatically presented questions behind impenetrable studio walls. But to other critics, the fascinating quality of *The Seventh Seal* seems to lie in what is *not* explained, in its allusive imagery and stylized rather than realistically conceived characters. One such critic is Peter John Dyer; another is filmmaker Eric Rohmer, whose approach is that of a semiologist but whose review of the film also emphasizes its visual beauty, its realistic landscapes, its theme of skepticism residing "in the opaqueness of appearances."

Although it seems likely that many viewers of *The Seventh Seal* have responded favorably to the film because they recognized in it an already established artistic pattern, several critics have taken Bergman to task for offering the spectators such a shortcut to aesthetic enjoyment. Swedish reviewers in particular have argued against the many literary and cinematic borrowings in the film. In Sweden *The Seventh Seal* became part of *kulturdebatten,* involving such nonfilm critics as Ivar Harrie and Professor John Landquist. Harrie preferred Bergman's *Wood Painting* as a play to *The Seventh Seal* as a film because in the former the language was allowed to carry the full impact of Bergman's imagination. Landquist, on the other hand, wrote off Bergman as a creative artist; to him *The Seventh Seal* was mostly borrowed and edited Strindberg. He saw special references to Strindberg's two plays *To Damascus,* a religious station drama, and *The Saga of the Folkungs,* a history play set in the fourteenth century which uses the motifs of the Black Death, the Apocalypse, and self-flagellation.

On the whole, Swedish critics showed considerable uncertainty in dealing with Bergman's film. They realized that it was different from anything else in the Swedish cinema *at the time* and they

---

[7] In the U.S.A., *Four Screenplays of Ingmar Bergman* (Simon and Schuster, N.Y., 1960) has been a popular text in literature courses.

seemed almost startled and uncomfortable by its visual beauty and its careful composition. In distrusting their own response to *The Seventh Seal* they looked eagerly for a prototype and found it in the classical Swedish film of the twenties, especially the works of Victor Sjöström. They frequently pointed to Sjöström's *The Phantom Carriage*, in which the main character struggles with the personified figure of Death, but they ignored the fact that in Sjöström's film (as in Selma Lagerlöf's novel upon which it is based) the issue is basically moral rather than metaphysical.

As is to be expected, the literary-verbal aspects of *The Seventh Seal* only occasionally became a crucial issue in foreign criticism: subtitles tend to reduce the scope and impact of spoken dialogue. But in Sweden Bergman as the author of *The Seventh Seal* was often called a *pekoralist* (bad stylist).[8] Foremost among those criticizing Bergman for his use of a pseudoliterary language was Harry Schein, until recently head of the Swedish Film Institute and now chairman of the board. In his essay entitled "Bergman, the Poet," Schein maintains that Bergman's talent is exclusively that of the creator of the cinematic sequence, who would have made a better film if he had pruned his dialogue of literary ambitions and left it at a nonliterary level with neutral lines like "May I offer you a bowl of milk" or "Can you show me the way to the Church?"

That critics who share Bergman's metaphysical vision would be favorably inclined to *The Seventh Seal* is hardly surprising. In France, the United States, and Latin America, that is, in countries less indifferent to religion than Scandinavia, Bergman has touched a very personal chord. But for an agnostic like Harry Schein, the religious search of Antonius Block would be of minimal interest, as I suspect it is to the majority of Swedes. Even so, Schein was willing to search for the film's impact on the public, beyond that of creating a sense of philosophical comradeship.

However, such efforts have rarely been made by equally nonreligious British critics of *The Seventh Seal*. Although Peter Cowie and, more recently, Robin Wood have done their best, in monograph studies, to promote an understanding of Bergman's films,

---

[8] It is amusing to contrast this view with one held by the reviewer in *The Scotsman* after *The Seventh Seal* was shown at the Edinburgh festival in August 1957: "The excellent English subtitles suggest that it [the original] has been written in dramatic blank verse, entirely suited to the period." *The Scotsman*, Aug. 23, 1957, p. 9.

they are far from typical of the British response to *The Seventh Seal*. Reviewers in *The New Statesman, The Spectator,* and in such diametrically opposed newspapers as *The Sunday Times* and *The Daily Worker* all seem to agree with Caroline Blackwood in her 1958 *Encounter* essay about some of Bergman's films of the fifties. Charging that Bergman is too Gothic and too rhetorical, Miss Blackwood concludes that his "cinematic fragments" get lost in "all the messy smorgasbord of his hysterical whimsical ideas."

Even though *The Seventh Seal* has always aroused strong reactions for or against Bergman, relatively few critics have paid close attention to its quality as film. I was delighted to come across James F. Scott's article on "Bergman in the 1950s" because it seemed to deal with some of the questions that need to be raised in any analysis of *The Seventh Seal*: Is the rhythm of the film effective? Does a kinetic pattern emerge which involves character and setting, conflict and point of view, mood and tempo?

Part of our difficulty in approaching *The Seventh Seal* may have to do with the fact that in this film Bergman is partly doing something which we traditionally consider the domain of literature: he is attempting to capture imaginatively a conceptual consciousness, that of the intellectual knight Antonius Block. Since he uses "plotted" storytelling (as against the "impromptu" cinema of some avant-garde and documentary filmmakers) with a beginning, a middle, and an end, it is tempting to use Aristotelian principles of evaluation. But we cannot really approach film as though it were an extension of traditional drama, even if film happens to follow a pattern that seems to correspond to the old dramatic one of exposition, climax, and denouement. The problem in analyzing storytelling cinema, Robert Gessner has said, is to realize that dramaturgy has been adapted to new forms of visualization, which have special movements.[9] To become meaningful, plot and themes in a film such as *The Seventh Seal* must at least to some degree be related to the orchestrated build-up of its sequences. The impact of the philosophical problems of Bergman's film cannot really be evaluated until we recognize to what extent its fragmented composition, which has annoyed a good many critics, may be part of a cinematic rhythmic pattern whereby moments of intellectual probing are juxta-

[9] Robert Gessner, *The Moving Image* (New York: E. P. Dutton & Co., 1970), pp. 17 ff.

posed to moments of great visual drama. Does the main theme of man's frustration in the face of eschatological matters emerge clearly because it is presented not only in the knight's constant questioning of Death and of Tyan, the girl who is burnt as a witch, but also in such emotionally tense sequences as that of plague-stricken Raval dying alone in the forest or of Death sawing off the tree in which Skat, the actor, has taken refuge? Would the secondary motif of the dilemma of the artist intrigue us if it were limited to the church painter's cynical remarks about his work and not given another dimension by the tortuous pantomime performance of Jof doing his bear dance in the tavern? And would the silence of God become an evident and awesome reality if it were defined merely through the knight's verbal outbursts of despair, without the desolate opening shot of the film in which a single bird moves silently against a cold leaden sky? [10]

It would appear today that any ultimate analysis of *The Seventh Seal* must take into account the extent to which Bergman has succeeded in creating a series of balances—light and dark, long shots and close-ups, dissolves and sudden cuts, idyllic moods and shock effects. More attention must be paid to the episodic, almost vignette-like structure of the film and to Bergman's juxtaposition of scenes of comic burlesque and hysterical frenzy, such as Skat's humorous seduction of Lisa while Jof and Mia execute a song about a world out of balance, a scene which is immediately followed by the train of screaming flagellants. Future students of Bergman will, hopefully, deal in greater depth with the structural aspects of the film, so that we may understand more fully the real impact of *The Seventh Seal.*

[10] Reviewers of Bergman's film have not always agreed upon what kind of bird it is that appears in the opening sequence. Bergman's own script refers to it as a seagull. Andrew Sarris and Harry Schein call it a hawk. Amedée Ayfre sees it as a Johannic eagle. It is a sea-eagle.

Meeting with Ingmar Bergman
by JEAN BÉRANGER

Wearing his legendary maroon beret, his cheeks darkened by a several-days-old beard that is to grow longer and thicker, Ingmar Bergman has just begun shooting his twentieth film, Ansiktet (The Face). *The takes proceed at good speed: I have hardly time to put my questions to him.*

—*You shoot ten times as fast as French filmmakers!*

—For a long time now I have noticed that the first take is almost always the best. After that the actors become impatient or tired: their gestures and their intonations show the effect of this. That's why, whenever possible, I prefer to confine myself to one or two takes.

—*Are you completely recovered from your illness?*

—It made me terribly tired. It's always that ulcer which I've had for twenty years now. It used to make its presence felt every spring and every fall. But for the last two or three years it has bothered me only in the springtime. But it is always on a fixed date: from the beginning of the month of April. Then I take advantage of it and retire to a hospital. And during my recovery I decide on the focus of my new scenario. I've always four or five synopses in front of me and it's during that period that I choose which one I shall attack.

I DETEST FESTIVALS

—*Many of your French admirers were very disappointed at not being able to meet you at Cannes.*

"Rencontre avec Ingmar Bergman" by Jean Béranger. From Cahiers du Cinéma, *no. 88 (October 1958):12–20. Reprinted by permission of Grove Press, Inc. Translated from the French by Birgitta Steene.*

—I too regret not having made the acquaintance of all those young critics. They seem to carry to the cinema the same love that I do. All that is written in your country on the subject of film interests me immensely. It also happens to take me by surprise sometimes. The way of viewing things is so different from one country to another that foreigners attach ideas to my person and my works which would not have occurred to me.

At any rate, you know how much I detest festivals and their glitter. I've always had a horror of the mundane. Next time I go to France it will be as a private person. I shall send you a note after my arrival and we shall go to the cinematèque and ask Langlois to show us the numerous European films of the last few years that I've not had a chance to see. We are very poorly served here: only the American production is presented to us with any regularity.

After arranging the last shot of the morning, we go to the studio canteen. We will now be able to talk in private for an entire hour. I learn from Bergman that in the next season some of his old films will be sent to Paris.

MY MASTERS ARE SWEDISH

—I admit that that annoys me. These "packages" will be shown in the most complete disorder, and it is not good policy for me to have my early works shown before my last ones.

It's not that I automatically denounce all my old films. There are quite simply some that I'd no longer wish to make or that I'd at least deal with in a different way.

—*Next winter a Paris cinema is going to show* Secrets of Women.

—Well, that one I still like well enough. But it's not the same with all my early films: I discover today a number of lacunæ and certain puerilities.

—*Were they not influenced by the prewar realistic French school?*

—Especially *A Ship to India.* When I was eighteen I admired Carné and Duvivier very much: those films had the charm of the exotic to us Swedes.

—*And Renoir?*

—Unfortunately the majority of his films have never been shown in Scandinavia and I've seen practically nothing by him.

—*It has been thought that there are certain points of resemblance between your* Smiles of a Summer Night *and his* Rules of the Game.

—I've never seen *Rules of the Game*. I terribly regret that. I hope that, thanks to Langlois, I shall be able to make up for all the deficiencies in my cinematic education when I come to Paris.

—*Do you think you have been influenced by the Italian neo-realism?*

—Very little, except perhaps with regard to *Port of Call*. We've seen very few Italian films here: I remember above all *Umberto D.*

—*You confided to me last year that of all your films you preferred* Illicit Interlude. *That opinion really surprised many of my fellow countrymen who place on top such works as* The Naked Night *and* The Seventh Seal.

—I prefer *Illicit Interlude* for very personal reasons. I made *The Seventh Seal* with my brain, *Illicit Interlude* with my heart. A part of my youth will forever be attached to that story: it was originally a little short story, which I wrote when I was seventeen. The scenario for *Torment* is also very close to my heart for similar reasons.

—*One has spoken, apropos of* The Seventh Seal, *of an influence from* Orphée.

—I consider *Orphée* one of the most beautiful French films ever made, at least of those that I've seen. I liked less *Beauty and the Beast,* which seemed to me too contrived. And to speak of a German influence is to commit an inaccuracy. The silent Swedish masters— imitated in their own time by the Germans—they alone have inspired me, in the very first place Sjöström whom I consider one of the greatest filmmakers of all times.

THE MAGICIAN AND THE MEDICAL DOCTOR

—*To what stream of inspiration do you attach* The Face,[1] *which you are shooting at the moment?*

—If you want, to the cycle of *The Seventh Seal*. The plot unfolds in a nineteenth-century milieu. A disciple of Mesmer (Max von Sydow) presents himself to a quiet bourgeois family and begins to exercise his gifts as a magician. A medical doctor with a deeply skeptical mind forms his antithesis.

—*We find the same dichotomy in* The Seventh Seal *and represented by the same actors.*

—As for Naima Wifstrand, who was the charming old chatelaine

---

[1] [Released in the U.S. in 1959 as *The Magician*.]

in *Smiles of a Summer Night,* she embodies the manner of a witch. That astonishing actress is now seventy years old. She made her debut in musicals more than half a century ago and she can still show proof of a vitality and a talent that could serve as an example to many young actresses. The rest of the cast comprises Bibi Andersson, Ingrid Thulin, Lars Ekborg (the young main actor in *Monika*), Åke Fridell, Bengt Ekerot (who played Death in *The Seventh Seal*), and Birgitta Pettersson (who made her debut with Arne Mattsson as the little girl in *Salka Valka*). As in almost all my films, Gunnar Fischer remains my chief photographer (he is also a remarkable illustrator of children's books). The musical score is by Erik Nordgren.

—*There was no music in* Brink of Life.

—Because I wanted the style of the film to be extreme. *The Face,* on the other hand, will be like *The Seventh Seal,* where Nordgren's score sometimes had the tone of suffering.

—*Was the subject matter of* Brink of Life *imposed upon you?*

—Not in the least. I liked very much the short story by Ulla Isaksson from which it was taken. Her theme resembles the one I had sketched briefly in certain parts of *Thirst* and *Secrets of Women,* dealing with the ceremony of childbirth. Besides, for two or three years we planned to make that film, Ulla and I.

—*Your father is, I believe, a chaplain at the Swedish court. May I ask what he thinks of your work?*

—My father has always left me completely free to think as I wish. He is a profoundly religious man. But he appreciates that I have to find my own track, and he has never wanted to raise the least objection to my judgments; he has shown a certain indifference to most of my old films. But he liked *The Seventh Seal* a great deal. He knows that I never say what I don't think sincerely. And note that I believe in God but not in the Church, Protestant or any other. I believe in a superior idea that we call God. I want to and have to. I believe it is absolutely necessary. Integral materialism could only lead humanity to an impasse without warmth.

TWENTY-THREE THEATER PLAYS

—*Your activity in the theater is very important, I believe.*

—It lasts about seven to twelve months. Every winter I produce many plays for the Municipal Theaters in Malmö and Göteborg.

—*After your filmography I would like to list all the plays that you have produced.*

—There are too many. And I would no doubt fail myself to make that list without omissions or errors in the chronology. You see, I've now set up plays for more than twenty years. I started when I was just a student. To be sure, I have explored Strindberg in particular. As for the French repertory, I've a very great admiration for Molière. Especially *Don Juan.*

I also have a great passion for Racine, but no translation of his plays into Swedish is really satisfactory. Our language remains very awkward with alexandrines. On the other hand, we possess excellent translations of Shakespeare. I've set up *A Midsummer Night's Dream, The Merchant of Venice,* and *Macbeth,* in three revivals and each one with an entirely different *mise en scène.* Of all the plays by that author I prefer without doubt *Macbeth.*

—*Do you prefer the theater or the cinema?*

—It's difficult to say. They are forms of expression that are at the same time very different and yet very close to each other. In one way, however, I think I prefer the theater: one can better control the mechanical subtleties.

—*You told me in an earlier conversation that you took the scenario for* The Seventh Seal *from a play written a few years earlier.*

—That's exactly right. It was called *Wood Painting.* It was very short, very impressionistic.

—*How many plays have you written?*

—Twenty-three or twenty-four, the first one at the age of seventeen. But I've only had six of those produced or published, among them *Dagen slutar tidigt* [*The Day Ends Early*], *Mig till skräck* [*To My Terror*] and *Rakel och biografvaktmästaren* [*Rachel and the Cinema Doorman*]. As for the rest, I prefer to keep them in my drawer.

—*To make films of them?*

—That's not very likely. I don't believe they are very good . . . and, then, my preoccupations have become modified.

FIDELITY TO SWEDEN

—*It's been said that after your success at Cannes and at Berlin, you've received offers to make films outside of Sweden.*

—I've received a few from everywhere. From France, Germany,

America, even Russia. The Germans wanted to hire me to make *A Doll's House,* after the play by Ibsen. The Americans have proposed to bring me to Hollywood to make an adaptation of Turgenev's *First Love.* But I don't want to make films anywhere but in Sweden. Look what happened to Sjöström and Stiller when they became expatriots. An artist cannot express himself fully and thereby succeed in touching the public in other countries except by remaining attached to all the particularities of his native soil. And besides, here my producers leave me with my hands completely free. It wasn't always like that. I've had to fight for a long time to arrive at that privileged position. Sometimes I've even shot works on commission, for example *It Couldn't Happen Here.* I hope that film will never be shown in France. It is scanty and hollow. I also make commercial films. Money is not for me the most important thing. But like everybody I have to pay my debts. And in summing up, it is probably more honest to make commercials than feature films that don't inspire you.

At present I'm really considered somewhat of a "rare bird." It's unpleasant from certain points of view but it doesn't affect my freedom of inspiration. I may do all I want, all that I may wish to do. Gunnar Fischer and I understand each other intuitively. I always work with the same material; I know by heart all the intricacies of our studios and laboratories. Likewise I use most of my actors from the City Theater in Malmö. Why should I prostitute myself elsewhere? Here I really have all the working instruments I wish to have. The air I breathe is that which has permitted me to believe and form myself. Why should I become unfaithful to it?

The Swedish cinema has finally succeeded in retrieving its secrets, lost for a long time. We can no longer permit ourselves to lose them a second time. If the producers in other countries wish to work with me, they should come here to do so and find a common ground of understanding with my real producers. I feel that I still have a lot to say, about the universe and about mankind. But I also feel that I could not really say it well except by talking about Sweden and about the Swedes.

Ingmar Bergman:
Craftsman and Visionary
by MARIANNE HÖÖK

Like the coachman Antonsson in *The Magician,* we become—unless we are the kind of people for whom magic fails—bound by Ingmar Bergman's magic. And just as it happens with Antonsson, it sometimes happens that we are afterwards overwhelmed by feelings of aggression because we've let ourselves become hypnotized. When, on reconsidering, we analyze what we've already swallowed, we may be overcome by a need for self-defense which manifests itself as intensely if not as violently as the strong coachman's. Bergman violates the spectator spiritually—his art can't be described any more simply than that. The creation of Antonsson and his reactions indicates a profound knowledge of the audience. The alienation of the artist which Bergman brings out so strongly is possibly based on the fact that he recognizes the ambivalence with which his movies have been received. This attitude toward the Bergman phenomenon —repulsion and, at the same time, recognition of the qualities of the films—in its own way indicates how engaging Bergman is as an artist. It is certain that he brings not peace but war. He himself, adroit in the art of rationalizing after the fact, emphasizes that film, his film, is intended to speak to the emotions without detouring through the intellect. Unfortunately it isn't possible to divide the audience into emotional and intellectual segments, only inviting the benevolent parts. At any rate, much of the tension and drama around Bergman's person and films are connected with the fact that the spectator gets drawn into a conflict which creates anxiety.

From Ingmar Bergman *by Marianne Höök (Stockholm: Bonniers, 1962), pp. 162–173. Reprinted by permission of Charlotte Sachs, M.D. Translated from the Swedish by Yvonne Sandström. [Editor's title.]*

What makes Bergman unique as a filmmaker? With the possible exception of Chaplin, Bergman has made the longest series of completely personal movies in the history of filmmaking. He is one of the few artists in films who can be judged the same way we judge a composer or a painter; his collected works determine his profile and his personal myth as far as *form and content* are concerned. Consequently, the attempt made here to examine his works is similar to the study of an author, although the viewpoint applied to Bergman isn't a literary one. If the important feature in, for example, the artistic profile of an Eisenstein is the montage, and in a Cayatte his pathos for justice, while in de Sica only the initiate can say where de Sica leaves off and Savattini begins, with Bergman it's the recurring dramatic motifs in his films that show who he is.

Bergman is an author with film as his natural means of expression. His brilliant talent is for script-writing *in combination with* directing, that is, for authorship in film. His genius is not narrative, hardly even descriptive, for the people in his movies have often been marionettes with fixed qualities, morality play characters disguised as humans. His greatness lies in dramatic vision, a dramatic-poetic vision which is a tool for the personal magic of the film author. At his best, Bergman is a genuine myth maker; much can be read into his myths. There's scope enough to fulfill everyone's need for interpretation, and everyone can find something on the shelf which is within his reach.

This unique ability to create myth would hardly have had a chance to develop in a different cultural climate and under a different system of film production. The Swedish production system is an essential ingredient in the picture of Bergman as filmmaker, and, combined with the time of his appearance, his own particular kind of talent, his energy, and his stubbornness, it has led to success. And once he had achieved success, Bergman had the opportunity to become even more ruthlessly personal.

The peculiarity of the Swedish production system is its small size —it is more cottage craft than industry—where everyone knows everyone else, in a climate where profit estimates, which are unreliable anyway as far as the movies are concerned, are replaced by sympathies and antipathies, arbitrary gambles for good *and* bad. After the First World War the Swedish film industry was in a boom period which made it possible for some individual producers to indulge themselves in occasional experimental extravagance. Production costs were modest, even considering the restricted circumstances, while production quantity was relatively large during the forties and fifties. About forty movies a year were made, a number that was reduced by more than half in the face of the assault of television after 1956. Had Ingmar Bergman arrived simultaneously with television, the progress of his development would have been different.

Ingmar Bergman was young, talented, and useful. He could write scripts, and Swedish film had suffered from a constant lack of scriptwriters. He also wanted to and was able to direct. Such a double function, however, was not customary; it was regarded as a somewhat reprehensible assumption of multiple duties. Therefore it took a surprisingly long time before Bergman had the opportunity to exercise these functions simultaneously. Bergman only emerged when he was able to effect the combination of script and direction in personal freedom, independent of industry. It's impossible to separate out what is script and what is direction, since what may appear to be superior direction is often found already embodied in the script, where the part as written is amazingly close to the image projected by the actor.

Bergman's problems of belief and his view of man attract more interest than do his pictorial sense and camera work. Through the years, Bergman has achieved a simplicity of form which—even if it has been a case of making a virtue of necessity—is geared to what he has to say. More and more he relies on the close-up, the face—and the spoken word. Even the form of the early movies was palpably and indiscriminately eclectic. There were influences from German expressionism, from Swedish lyrical romanticism, and from the French movies of the thirties. *Prison* and *Waiting Women* still exhibit a collection of samples of different cinematic styles. In the Frost segment in *The Naked Night* Bergman makes his most original and successful experiment in form.[1] But for some inexplicable reason it remains an isolated occurrence. From this point on, Bergman uses the camera as if he didn't use it. He differs from, for example, the new Frenchmen in that no playful impulses are engendered in him by technical possibilities. He wants the camera to be noticed as little as possible. He is always primarily the man of

[1] [This is a reference to the opening sequence where the clown Frost is the dominant character.]

the theater who distrusts technical shortcuts, only relying on the human being and on the spoken word.

He is more interested in the composition of pictures than in the possibilities of camera movement. This manifests itself in his pre-dilection for silhouette effects and in the inner tension in the com-ponents of the picture. His montage is not daring and does not aim for surprising visual effects. Nor does it aim for the synthesis among montage elements which, in film, corresponds to what can be read between the lines in good literature. Instead, his montage is char-acterized by a strong rhythmic sense both internally and externally. The external rhythm of the films is often simply accomplished with alternating comic and dramatic episodes, as if Bergman wanted to offer different segments of his audience what they wanted or could be assumed to want. The internal rhythm of the films, which is less accessible to analysis, is essential for the total effect and unity of form which is typical of Ingmar Bergman's best work. He has a pronounced sense of color effect in black and white. In its enormous whiteness, *Smiles of a Summer Night* possesses all the nuances of a color movie and a joy in the rendering of the material which is seldom found in film but often in painting. *Wild Strawberries* ex-hibits a still greater capacity for color variation. Here Bergman works in three color scales: the dark and threatening drama of the nightmares, the certainty of everyday reality in the framing narra-tive, and the white elegy of the youthful dreams.

One element in Bergman's films which has gone unnoticed—in spite of the fact that this element undoubtedly contributes greatly to the total effect—is his treatment of sound. His musicality and auditory supersensitivity have been spoken of before. Both these qualities affect his treatment of sounds. Bergman movies are very seldom accompanied by the standard symphonic music which, at least before, seemed to be the same for all movies. His musical aids are sparingly but subtly inserted and indicate a collaboration be-tween director and composer unusually intimate for movie condi-tions. But even in Bergman's *Brink of Life,* where no music is used, his supreme auditory talent is evident. *Brink of Life* is accompanied by documentary sounds: footsteps, doors closing, glass clinking, metal clanking. Bergman's supersensitivity to sound is here con-sciously inserted into the movie and assaults the audience with strong and meaningful effects.

Even if Bergman lacks interest in or disposition for original pictorial creation, he has been carrying on industrious research. He has acquired an extensive collection of film copies for his personal use, primarily Swedish classics from the Sjöström–Stiller era. For a couple of years, Bergman, together with his coworkers, has been making a systematic study of the technique of color movies from all aspects. This study is preparatory work for the color movie which he will make sooner or later. Bergman is not the kind of cinematic artist who relies on inspiration and improvisation, except when he is well prepared. He wants to capture the moment before it has become worn and the bloom is off it, but this takes careful practice. Bergman speaks of the short minute during the whole day's filming when the production catches fire and comes alive. That minute isn't to be worn down by retakes and excessive repetition. Rather it is, for him, a question of putting both the technical apparatus and the actors into a condition of concentrated vitality. He seems to function as the generator in his productions, as if they lived on his personal emission of power.

The two photographers with whom Bergman has most often collaborated are Gunnar Fischer and Sven Nykvist. Gunnar Fischer has worked in twelve of his films, among them *Smiles of a Summer Night, Wild Strawberries,* and *The Magician.* As a professional, as a personality, and as an artist Gunnar Fischer has functioned as a cocreator with sensitive perception of Bergman's intentions and a similar attitude, strongly entering into the spirit of the work. He has not been wax for Bergman to mold; he has rather been an independent but at the same time well-synchronized artistic collaborator. Sven Nykvist has made *The Naked Night* (together with Hilding Bladh) and, in Bergman's later production, *The Virgin Spring, Through a Glass Darkly,* and *Winter Light.* Nykvist functions more as a direct medium for Bergman. He does not take as large a personal place as Fischer, which may possibly explain the change of photographer in the later movies. By way of comparison it can be said that Fischer gives the stronger character portrayals. His lighting and close-ups in, for example, *The Magician,* are inextricably bound up with his conception of Bergman and of Bergman's movies.

It is in the nature of the case that such an extremely personal artist as Bergman is not, once he has matured, subject to tangible influence either with reference to motifs or to aesthetics. Neither does he start a movement. Since his international breakthrough Bergman's influence can now and then be traced in French and

Italian movies, but only as occasional and isolated phenomena. Thus Rolleau's *The Witches of Salem* was very closely related to the Bergman–Fischer movies. Bergman has also left an imprint on some of the new Poles, on Kawalerowic's *Mother Johanna of the Angels* and Wajda's *Samson*. In Fellini's *La Dolce Vita* the segment of the castle at night, for example, shows a certain similarity in form to Bergman; this is also true of the long final dialogue in Antonioni's *La Notte*.

Bergman's influence on the French new wave is on a different plane from that of method and form. It is surprising that direct manifestation of personality has been lacking in French film for so many years, aside from such industrially unimportant exceptions as Cocteau. It is reasonable to assume that a latent need must have existed. That this need has not been satisfied must be connected with the structure of the French film industry.

With its star system, which had reached dimensions far out of proportion to its market, French film had arrived at a dead end during the fifties. In this situation the encounter with Bergman must have been liberating for the French film authors as well as for the French film industry. Here was someone who showed that you could manifest yourself in film under economically conventional and respectable forms. For the young Frenchmen this must have seemed more industrially than artistically liberating. Bergman's most remarkable accomplishment lies in the extent to which the manifestation of personality in his movies has contributed to greater freedom for film authors.

As far as the conception of the movies is concerned we only have Bergman's own account to guide us. He has drawn parallels between the experiences of childhood and pictures on a window shade, the landscape of damp spots on the ceiling, the fascination of a wallpaper pattern, and Grandmother's picture of Venice, which suddenly seemed to come alive. It is evident that Bergman starts with a problem, a plot that needs solving. It starts with a picture, a situation. Bergman himself says:

A face, strongly and suddenly illuminated, a hand raised in a gesture, a square at dusk with a couple of old women sitting on a bench with a bag of apples between them. Or an exchange of words, two people who suddenly say something in voices completely their own, perhaps they are turned away, I can't see their faces, but still I am forced to listen to them, to wait for them until they come back again and repeat the same words without significance but carrying a secret tension, a tension I'm still ignorant of, but which has an insidious sweetness. The lighted face, the gesture of the hand raised in conjuration, the old women in the square, and the few insignificant words—they are caught like glittering fish in my net, or rather, I myself have been caught in a net whose construction I'm happily ignorant of.

In regard to the craftsman aspect of scriptwriting Bergman has his extraordinary work discipline to support his inspirations. He writes his daily quota at established times, delivers on the promised date, and is receptive to the opinions of producers, or at least he was receptive during Carl Anders Dymling's time. While he is strictly occupied with the making of one movie, it often happens that ideas for another one start invading him. Bergman has a flowing richness of ideas and always has a handful of themes he's experimenting with, finished and half-finished ideas for movies. It is a peculiarity of Bergman's talent as an author that he never succeeded in fulfilling his intentions as a writer for the theater. For this, psychological passion, among many other things, is a prerequisite and Bergman has a more clinical kind of interest in man and the behavior of man. His sensibility is directed toward what human beings can do to each other, how they touch each other, and how emotional groupings arise and manifest themselves, in approximately the same way as one might admire the beauty values of crystalline forms or the pattern of iron filings around a magnet. He has an X-ray eye—quite unschooled—for the emotional charge of human beings. At least when he was younger, Bergman had an almost itchy-fingered desire to put people into affect, to make them shout, weep, let themselves go. He has a highly developed ability to catch the quiverings in the relations between people, to perceive atmospheric disturbances. But all of this—this extremely special kind of giftedness—does not mean that a real interest in man or pronounced love of man can be ascribed to Bergman. Thus a recurrent motif in his films is accusations and self-accusations of indifference, egoism, and contempt for mankind: an indifference which is its own punishment because it fosters isolation.

No doubt a certain degree of egocentricity is a necessity for an artist—an unclouded faith in the significance of his own experience is at least required. Egocentricity can be both an escape and a protection in order to keep intact and provide opportunities for work. But when the artist's own independence is girded about with walls, the result is that the walls don't just keep unauthorized persons out. They also shut in. There are examples of this in any artist's biography. Bergman's guarding of himself and his own has taken new form since he has become a worldwide success, something which can be a terrible human misfortune. He no longer has as much use for aggressiveness, since he has the power of getting his working and personal life arranged the way he wants it. But he seems to concern himself only with those aspects of existence which he has, once and for all, staked out a claim to. He does not go outside his own pattern, and this implies an artistic limitation.

We have to assume that it is this indifference to human beings, except when seen as marionettes, which is the reason Bergman does not take a stand and consequently is continually accused of intellectual dishonesty and indifference to social issues. His kind of dramatic feeling is not directed toward setting up problems and trying out different solutions. Generally speaking, it isn't the situation as soluble problem which interests him; neither does he show a fatalistic weariness over the impossibility of solving any problem whatsoever. His interest lies in the situation, the constellation, and in the play of dramatic forces within it. The choice of position which is unavoidable in drama he gets from conceptions of faith, marked by the anxiety-producing rigor of his early experiences. Bergman's dilemma consists in the fact that he has an extraordinary sensitivity to people and to their mutual circumstances as well as a brilliant ability to render these sensitivities visible. But at the same time his field of vision is restricted by his lack of common humanity. He is the manipulator who makes the marionettes move.

His brilliance as a director of actors resides exactly in this ability to stand aside and listen. It is evident that Bergman never transforms actors in his movies. He chooses the actor already at the stage of script ideas and develops the part according to the personality of the actor. He never goes against the intention of the actor himself or the actor's image but instead uses them as building blocks and cement for the part. Since he has opportunity to hand pick his artists and to get the ones that for him are the best and most suitable, this technique means that everything which the actor himself embroiders on the custom-made part contributes to developing the part in the desired direction. Bergman is very intent on capturing and preserving all those little natural traits born and fostered at the meeting between his script and the actor around whom he has spun his character. His ability to direct actors is to a large extent an ability to recreate conditions.

This means that Bergman only rarely discusses their parts with his actors and that he often neglects to make purely intellectual analyses. What he does during his productions is to create an atmosphere of concentrated attention and to pull all those involved in the production, even technicians, into his personal whirling movements. Through working so intimately with the actor's image and through his enormous assurance and his sensitivity to what people have inside them, Bergman succeeds in getting astonishing results where other directors don't get beneath the surface.

Ingmar Bergman in the 1950s
by JAMES F. SCOTT

During the last two decades filmmaker Ingmar Bergman has been busily making his name one of the best known in Europe and America. No doubt there is a trace of faddishness in his success, since certain idiosyncrasies of his vision have endeared him to those who luxuriate in their own neuroses. Whatever his limitations, however, his accomplishments are genuine. Most obviously, he has brought to the cinema a sense of form which is exceptionally acute. It is of more particular significance, though, that Bergman's very specialized talent—his capacity to bring fantasy, dream, and myth once again within the area of major cinematic interest—constitutes a valuable counterpoise to the dominantly realistic, socially oriented film of Western Europe.

The long-standing sociological bias of European cinema makes Bergman's subjectivist style crucially important to the further development of film technique. Premature in their technical aspirations, the early expressionist ventures of France and Germany, epitomized in *The Cabinet of Dr. Caligari,* gave way in the middle twenties to the meticulous realism which has since dominated the work of Europe's best-known directors, Cocteau and Dreyer perhaps excepted. While the stark detail of Pabst's *The Joyless Street* caught the imagination of depression-ridden Europe, several distinguished Soviet directors were showing how well the film would adapt to convey the content of dialectical materialism. During the thirties, moreover, the influence of Eisenstein and Pudovkin loomed steadily larger, not only because of their penetrating writings upon cine-

"Ingmar Bergman in the 1950s" by James F. Scott. This essay is a slightly revised version of the author's "The Achievement of Ingmar Bergman," printed in The Journal of Aesthetics and Art Criticism 24, *no. 2 (December 1965): 263–70 Reprinted by permission of the author and* JAAC.

matography but equally as a result of the growing collectivist tendencies of Western culture. In the era of fascist challenge and socialist response, the director followed the lead of the philosopher in sensitizing his audience to the realities of mass movement, as maturing techniques of editing made montages and dissolves the ideal means to catch the fury of a street riot, the deployment of battalions, the squalor of a famine-haunted village.

These emphases, of course, were accelerated by World War II and its aftermath, as the haggard honesty of Italy's *neorealismo* reminds us. In their work of the postwar decade, Rossellini and de Sica, as well as Antonioni and Visconti, took their inspiration from the public world of burned cities and displaced masses, the shattered landscape where ignorant armies clashed by night. And though these artists have given most polished utterance to the upheaval of European reconstruction, their material differs only in degree from the works of lesser Continental directors who have addressed themselves to essentially the same phenomena. Nearly all have concentrated upon the response of the individual to some realistically rendered environment, the shaping of spirit accomplished within some institutional frame. Only quite recently has the drama of psychic reality begun to regain prestige.

Both tradition and disposition, however, have inclined the Swedish director to resist the idiom of documentary realism. Temperamentally introspective and the product of a prosperous, relatively static, politically neutralist culture, he has found little to excite him in *cinema engagé*. His inspiration derives instead from earlier achievements of his native Svensk Filmindustri, from the gothic world of Sjöström's *The Phantom Coach* and the psychoanalytical orientation of Sjöberg's cinematic *Miss Julie*. Bergman's theater is the inner world of the psyche, where need engenders desire or fear enervates will, where memory beclouds sight and reason struggles against madness. As would be expected, his apprenticeship to filmmaking has assumed the form of a continuing experiment with means to bring the revelations of the analyst's couch and the magician's stage convincingly before the camera.

It was during the 1950s that Bergman established himself as a major director and first found a mode acceptable to his subjectivist vision. This involved launching his career as a scriptwriter, recruiting his basic production team, and learning how to extract consistently expert performances from a choice ensemble of actors.

Bergman wrote his first original screenplay in 1948, for *Port of Call*,[1] though it was not until 1952 that he abandoned his off-and-on collaboration with Herbert Grevenius. *Port of Call* also occasioned Bergman's first contact with two key members of his technical staff, photographic director Gunnar Fischer and film editor Oscar Rosander. Fischer shot almost every Bergman picture of the next decade, while Rosander handled much of the cutting. The look of Bergman's films in the 1950s owes a great deal to the artistic preferences of these men, especially the photography of Fischer. The cadre of actors varies more widely, but typically includes Eva Dahlbeck, Harriet Andersson, and Gunnar Björnstrand (each making his first appearance with Bergman in 1952) as well as Max von Sydow, Bibi Andersson, and Ingrid Thulin, all of whom joined the troupe in the middle fifties. Although Bergman never reduces these actors to stereotypical presences (von Sydow, for instance, plays everything from a questing knight to a gas station attendant), he tends to cast them in somewhat predictable roles, as if to make them enflesh certain aspects of his private world. The mobile features and deep-set eyes of von Sydow ideally qualify him as the soul-searching Bergmanian hero, while the angular face and stiff carriage of Björnstrand turn him towards colder, more skeptical, more cynical roles. Harriet and Bibi Andersson tend to personify the distinction between sensuous and spiritual youthfulness, while Dahlbeck and Thulin provide Bergman with complex versions of feminine maturity. In the company of these technicians and performers, Bergman perfected the style which sets off his films of the fifties from those he would make in the following decade.

In technical terms, this style is disarmingly simple. Range and angle are supremely important, because Bergman uses gradual movements of the camera to exclude unwanted background material from his shots, thus allowing the changing composition of successive frames to define the shifting emotional responses of his characters. Montage also figures in the projection of the inner life, but not so prominently. Single inserts are much more common than elaborate optical mosaics. For his most sophisticated effects he prefers the

---

[1] Throughout the essay I will employ the American titles of Bergman's films, on the assumption that these are the most familiar. My citations of dialogue are from *Four Screenplays of Ingmar Bergman* (New York, 1960) and *The Virgin Spring* (New York, 1960), both translated by David Kushner and Lars Malmström.

dissolve, especially a very slow dissolve which retains the displaced image long enough to make its force operative in the new frame.

In transacting this interior revelation, Bergman has always depended heavily upon a small store of cinematically compelling images, remarkable both for the frequency with which they occur and for the variety amid sameness achieved in their use. The natural world in its seasonal changes; the stage or arena; the mirror or glass: these are the basic visuals of Bergman's films. Laden with traditional associations yet always reshaped by immediate dramatic contexts, these deceptively simple details define the various expressions of selfhood in its continuous encounter with nature and society. These images are truly symbols, for repetition invests them with more than literal expressiveness.

Few shots figure so prominently in Bergman's films as those of water, which through its power to reflect both form and light typically serves to control a larger body of outdoor imagery. The water image is central because it mediates between the phenomenal and the psychic world, suggesting not only the endless flux of experience but also the tendency of such experience to take color from the mental complexion of those undergoing it. Nearly always ambivalent, the image is both a natural absolute and a psychic variable. Hence in the last scene of *Secrets of Women* (1952), the open and expansive surface of the lake spread before the eloping lovers naturalistically represents the fluid possibilities of life available upon their escape from a restrictive environment. At the same time, however, the delicate moonlight silhouetting these exuberant innocents symbolizes their own naive infatuation, as is borne out in a bystander's comment upon the charming impermanence of romantic affection. A similar mergence of sea and skyscape operates to define the relationship between the young lovers of *Illicit Interlude* (1950). As their liaison develops, Bergman's camera hovers over scenes in which moving waters flash brilliantly with the glint of noonday sunshine, blinding and evanescent as the passion of the lovers it iconically resembles. And while the rhythm builds towards the accident which robs the heroine of her lover, the motif of quenched fire is extended in the blazing skyrockets whose downward trajectory is towards extinction in the sea. In cooperation with various seasonal backdrops, the water image continues to function in Bergman's later films. Witness the frozen landscape of *Winter Light* (1962).

Another metaphor to which Bergman shows great partiality is

that of the stage. Even when his protagonists are not professional actors, they continue to be players of roles. This point is frequently emphasized in photography which concentrates attention on some kind of enclosed area. Here the frail self seeks to assume some acceptable public posture, largely in the interest of its own psychic survival. The importance of role-playing is underscored in a sequence from *The Naked Night* (1953), which uses the circus arena as the stage for a fight between the clumsily candid circus-master and the wily thespian who has stolen his mistress. With his calculatedly graceful movements, the actor outmaneuvers and humiliates his adversary, not because he is the better man but because he is the better performer. Though the role he plays is knavish, it equips him to live successfully, if not honorably, in a world where personal identity is constantly threatened by the intrusive demands of others. One's public stance need not be perverse, though, as is shown in *The Magician* (1958) when Vogler triumphs over Vergérus. In the famous attic scene from this film, victory again lies with the actor, the showman who has planned his performance supremely well. But Vogler's sleight-of-hand is fundamentally a moral act, in that it explodes the cocksure positivism of his antagonist. When the man he supposed a corpse rises to life before his blurred vision, Vergérus finds his scientific posture crushed as completely as the broken spectacles Bergman's tracking camera picks up. At the moment of crisis, Vogler has played the role of conjurer more effectively than Vergérus the role of rational skeptic, and in this case the vanquished player is the less humanly admirable of the two. If these sequences make the significance of the stage metaphor seem ambiguous, the matter is appreciably clearer in *Winter Light*. From this film we understand that man constructs his various masks not so much to defeat others as to save himself. Indeed, he must strut and fret his hour upon the stage, whether or not his performance is even worthy of an audience. Thus it is with Parson Tomas, whose desperate effort to find spiritual insulation brings him finally to conduct a solemn vesper service within the sanctuary of his empty church. Like so many Bergmanian characters, doubting Tomas ritualizes his behavior as stage play and thereby reveals the strategy of personal defense embodied in its formalized pattern.

To the images of nature and art should be added the mirror or glass, for Bergman employs this visual detail to further the analysis of private emotions—sometimes to suggest the achievement of self-knowledge, more often to explore, ironically, its absence. The thematic metaphor of *Through a Glass Darkly* (literally translated, "as if in a mirror") is photographically central to all Bergman's work. Its operation is well illustrated in *Dreams* (1955), a film in which reflecting images objectify contrasting motifs of innocence and experience. For the giddy young model, Doris, whose journey to the city betokens complete commitment to her career, a short pause before the window of a jewelry shop perfectly reveals her sensuous ardor, a precondition of the gusto with which she faces the opening up of life. As she savors the array of precious stones, facial gestures caught in the glass fuse with the elegant display itself, creating an image which identifies her enthrallment with the plush expectations of a successful career. But the aging fashion designer who makes the trip with Doris entertains no such romantic illusion about herself. The elder woman's resignation to life's hopelessness is framed in a mirror image which superimposes her expressionless features upon a rain-spattered window, the droplets both visually and psychologically analogous to human tears. The image also projects her future, which, like the accidental splash of water, may promise much random motion but little significant change of pattern. The kind of camera work we see here is transparently simple, yet the more effective for its unpretentiousness. While dramatic realism places a mirror in the roadway, Bergman's mirrors stand before the human soul.

Of course, isolated details never make a great film, and Bergman's stature depends ultimately upon his ability to incorporate expressive images into larger dramatic patterns. When he is most successful, this rhythm is neither theatrical nor painterly, but arises from a grasp of the unique ontology of cinema: action is progressively interpreted and resolved in symbols of psychic life which develop naturally from the photographic surface. First attaining the proportions of greatness in *The Seventh Seal* (1956) and culminating in the masterful effects of *The Virgin Spring* (1959), Bergman's experiments in symbolic drama exemplify both the trials and the triumph of a director determined to harmonize graphic values and dramatic movement, visually projecting the spiritual energy of his protagonists while faithfully rendering the successive occasions which call it into being.

After achieving unqualified success with the stylized realism of *The Naked Night,* Bergman turned in the middle fifties to the more explicitly symbolic mode of *The Seventh Seal*. Developed from his own play, *Wood on Painting*, the film would seem foredoomed to be excessively theatrical. And it does, in fact, lean too heavily upon the static iconography of expressionist drama. In spite of Bergman's effort to create fluidity, the symbolic chess match remains slightly intrusive, occasionally interruptive of the action. The remarkable feature of *The Seventh Seal*, however, is the degree to which the director overcomes the implicit tendencies of his material. Throughout the film the physical texture of life surrounds us with oppressive density, almost demanding the soritical gamesmanship by which Antonius Block in his match with Death strives to master the chaos of experience. Nor do the several appearances of Death stand in frozen isolation from the human drama. Solid and imposingly alive (he even wields a saw), this allegoric figure is drawn into the natural landscape, while the apocalyptic tempest gathers in storm clouds whose substance seems perfectly tangible. Furthermore, Bergman minimizes the intrusiveness of directly expressionistic scenes through a careful modulation of tonal rhythm which prepares us for these exceptional chords. This results in interplay between the concrete visuals of camera reality and the symbolically staged mental processes of the doubt-haunted hero.

With praiseworthy neatness, Bergman immediately relates the expressionistic dimension of the film to dramatic action and scenic detail. The opening frames vividly portray the disenchanted Crusader who can no longer maintain his spiritual poise in a world limitlessly drab and relentlessly fluid, like the wash of the surf beside which he tries to pray. When saluted by Death, however, Block refuses to surrender until his mind has wrested some meaning from the purposeless flux of experience. There follows the beginning of the chess match, whose symbolic import is defined through superimposition. As the two players advance their king's pawns, the dissolve impresses the geometrically exact patterns of the chessboard upon the plastic, asymmetrical surface of the sea, thereby suggesting Block's eleventh-hour search for a logically structured philosophy to refurbish his shattered faith. The match with Death, we thus realize, will progress in a manner directly analogous to Block's heroic struggle against the spirit of negation that threatens his moral universe.

Having established his basic symbol, Bergman wisely refrains from further appeals to the chessboard until the intensity of the action has been permitted to mount, climax, and fade in a delicate decrescendo at the center of the film. We are reminded of the game when Block informs his confessor that he will defeat Death with "a combination of the knight and the bishop"—a plan illustrative of the protagonist's continuing loyalty to the feudal mystique. But while this allusion impresses its import upon us, we are carried forward to a crisis of action so powerful as to efface all sense of contrivance or artifice. Sound, timing, and pictorial composition cooperate to make Block's meeting with the self-torturing flagellants one of the most memorable in Bergman's films, the more so because it effectively alters the direction of the hero's quest for certitude. As this sequence begins, the gay song of dancers is drowned in the fearful chant of plague-stricken marchers, a counterpointing which leads naturally to the expressions of terror frozen into the faces of those awestruck by the grotesque procession. The chilling sound of whips and scourges is hushed during the oration of the sadistic monk who leads the penitents, but the horrific snap of the lash is again heard as the congregation resumes its pilgrimage amid swirls of incense which suffocates as many as it sanctifies. Before the marchers vanish, a long-range shot from high angle appropriately signifies a new perspective, the one Block has attained now by detaching himself intellectually from the company of the orthodox. Explosive action thus begets new perception, which leads, after a parallel climax in the subplot, to a gradual calming of the dramatic rhythm. Frenzied shrieks give way to pastoral hospitality as Block enters into a new covenant of friendship with the traveling performers. And at this moment the return to the static world of the chessboard comes as a dying fall which reverberates in solemn stillness.

Unfortunately, this rising and falling rhythm is not so well suited to the latter part of the film, since completion of the chess match necessitates interruption of the mounting pressure of catastrophe. Confronted with this problem, Bergman handles his material knowingly, but not quite successfully. To emphasize continuity, he omits the dissolve we expect as Block, after witnessing the deaths of Tyan and Raval, returns to the chessboard for the misplay which symbolically represents the spirit of hubris dramatized in scenes immediately preceding. There is also an attempt to make the symbolic interlude itself suspenseful, for Block's toppling of the chessmen is a stratagem to cover the escape of Jof and Mia. Skyscape montage interpolated as this pair leaves Block's company restores much of the energy lost at the chessboard, even if the effect of the compensatory insert smacks of deliberate inflation. In spite of these efforts, the closing sequences lack smoothness, a difficulty not quite offset by the subtly articulate facial gestures of von Sydow, which give Block's last prayers such authenticity. There remains a dramatic difficulty. At the last crucial moment the expressionistic stage is disturbingly separate from the urgently real world of storm and plague. Faults notwithstanding, Bergman exhibits bold imagination in the cinematic strategy of this film. But uncertainties of style suggest a lingering indebtedness to the theater, an as yet incomplete emancipation from the stage, which opens the way to further experiments in the presentation of spiritual phenomena.

As if unsatisfied with the somewhat contrived character of the symbolic chess match, Bergman sets out in his next film, *Wild Strawberries* (1957), to approximate more closely the exact texture of psychic life through the mode of dream. For this some will never forgive him, and there is no foolproof rejoinder to those who will not tolerate dreams anywhere except in their own beds. But to disparage the somnambulistic action is to miss the distinguishing virtue of the film—its commendably graphic presentation of the cerebral life of Isak Borg. Through a baroque profusion of images, we become active participants in his belated struggle to regain the imaginative vitality he has deliberately shunted aside, and the interest is more than clinical because the desperate compulsion driving the protagonist toward the polyvalent world of childhood is really the measure of his moral integrity. The only fault of the film, ironically (for I have never seen anyone mention it), is the treatment of the daylight world, the public landscape of contemporary Sweden. Here events succeed each other haphazardly, arbitrarily, forming a succession far more loosely arranged than the insubstantial pageant of Borg's mind. Bergman seems willing to tolerate all kinds of improbable incidents provided they help fill the hero's memory with resources for associative fantasy. If *The Seventh Seal* depends too heavily upon theatrical regimentation, *Wild Strawberries* too heavily favors the painterly, achieving its pictorial values at the expense of a strong narrative line. The flaws are not fatal, however, and thus the film reveals a further dimension of Bergman's cinematic creativity.

The most admirable feature of *Wild Strawberries* is Bergman's portrayal of tension and resolution in Borg's interior life. This is first done through skillful counterpointing of sound and scene, later through pictorial composition alone. The overexposed shots which give the opening sequence its hideous whiteness are reminiscent of German cinema, but the use of the sound track achieves an original effect. The posed remarks of the note-taking Professor Borg stand in sharp relief to the terrified groping of his somnambulist double. And though his conscious mind asserts "all I ask of life is to be left alone," Borg's sleep is deeply troubled by the sense of isolation. Emptiness and silence haunt the dreamer as he moves hesitantly past closed shutters and hasped windows to salute a faceless man whose body crumbles at a single touch. Dream logic continually presses the image of estrangement into new shapes until it receives its ultimate expression in Borg's witnessing his own funeral. Unconsciously, the lonely doctor has already pronounced himself dead, for his embittered emotional neutrality is clearly a living death. But the doctor, unreceptive to this instinctive wisdom, awakens determined to purge his demon with the brisk exercise of a drive.

In further dream sequences, Bergman artfully arranges the composition of his frames to establish the increasing completeness of Borg's absorption into the repressed environment of his psychic past. When he meets the dream figure of Sara, his voice dies before reaching her, implying that he still cannot speak the language of impulse. At this moment, the distance between the two characters is underscored in photography which places Borg in a separate picture plane, cut off from Sara first by a low wall of waving grass, later by portentous shadows. In the scene on the heath, however, after Borg has recognized the consequences of his unbending egoism, a calculatedly slow dissolve telescopes pictorial surfaces to assimilate the hero into a barren autumnal landscape. The anguish his growing self-knowledge entails is also incorporated into the fleeting image which shows his head trapped in the pincerlike clasp of a gnarled tree. But painful humiliation redeems the doctor as a human agent, qualifying him for the dream of paradise regained which concludes the film. Her hand clasped to his, Sara now leads Borg to the translucent waters of regeneration, over which the camera hovers until the final cut. Bergman has deftly followed the curvature of Borg's perception as he reclaims his power of imaginative sympathy.

These carefully wrought images of psychic reality are accomplished at considerable sacrifice to the dramatized life beyond the mind of

Borg. Coincidence and manipulation abound. Young Sara, the *anima* figure of Borg's dreams, seems magically to conjure her double who inhabits time present and accidentally encounters old Isak during the journey to Lund. Her eccentric companions, holding their protracted debate on the claims of reason and emotion, are authorial puppets too obviously representing rival forces in the hero's personality. Not even the public highway is uncluttered with Bergman's symbols. A careening automobile overturns as it passes, conveniently obliging the doctor to take its passengers into his charge and thus adding two essential characters to the gallery of his dream world. Contrivance lessens as the film progresses, and the final sequences seem perfectly credible. Borg's son Evald is a fully enfleshed character, and the academic ceremony, full of hothouse Latin and stodgy posturing, is a triumph of realistic comedy which sweeps away the creaking machinery so prominent earlier. The impressive recovery in the final scenes markedly increases the persuasiveness of *Wild Strawberries,* though we are still left with the sense that this work, for all its undoubted brilliance, takes less than sufficient account of the intractable data of experience.

After finishing *The Brink of Life* (1957) and *The Magician,* the latter a polished work in its own right, Bergman completed in 1959 what seems to me a genuine masterpiece, *The Virgin Spring.* Delegating the screenplay to Ulla Isaksson, whose script is adequate if uninspired, the director here surpasses all his earlier efforts to make the photographic image a vehicle of thematic import. Expertly foreshadowed, the miracle scene which consummates the symbolic pattern is not so theatrical as the chess match in *The Seventh Seal.* The shots are as fully expressive as those of *Wild Strawberries,* but leave no lingering flavor of preciousness. This latter accomplishment owes much to the promotion of Sven Nykvist to director of photography. "Bergman and I promised each other when we started *The Virgin Spring,*" says the veteran cameraman, "there would be no beauty effects." [2] But Bergman himself is responsible for the timing and rhythm which gracefully effects the difficult double climax essential to this drama of crime, vengeance, and regeneration.

The Virgin Spring begins with three contrasting scenes, introducing along with the central characters the basic images to be

[2] Sven Nykvist, "Photographing the Films of Ingmar Bergman," *American Cinematographer* (October 1962), p. 628.

elaborated in later sequences. Fire and darkness are immediately associated with the primitive, pagan world of impulsive hatred and suspicion, as Ingeri blows on glowing embers which flare to illumine her sullen features while she invokes Odin for redress of supposed injuries. But that her attraction to fire is not peculiar to servants of the deposed Viking divinity is shown in the next series of shots which reveals Töre and Märeta at their morning worship. Töre's wife seems almost to relish the hot wax which sears her arm as it drips from the sacramental candles burning in honor of Christ. In Märeta, hatred has been sublimated to quasi-religious masochism, though it retains its destructiveness. In contrast to the motif of fire, with its suggestions of malice and pain, the next shift of scene gives us the outdoor world and the first glimpse of flowing water, faintly anticipatory of the miraculous spring whose upsurge is the final image of regeneration. A hint of this rebirth theme is also injected into the dialogue when the servant Frida, amid sentimental caresses, renews the life of a young chick she "nearly stepped on . . . out there in the darkness."

With the introduction of Karin, Bergman initiates movement towards the film's first climax, the brutal rape and murder of this unwary traveler. Foreshadowings of impending disaster are carried in the outdoor imagery. Alternating high and low camera angles play off a backdrop of blooming flowers (with which Karin identifies herself by picking a bouquet) against a darkening sky of billowing thunderheads. Clear running water is muddied by the hooves of horses shortly before Karin, having forded the stream, silhouettes her brightly clad form against the impenetrable darkness of the forest. From the outset of the girl's journey, however, Bergman's long shots have continued to suggest ultimate reconciliation, as the soft focus in which distant landscapes are caught causes patches of light and dark, sun and shadow, to blend with one another.

The tempo of the film quickens from the moment Ingeri abandons Karin, Bergman accentuating the increased number of cuts with rapid changes of place, while the herdsmen entrap the heroine. Individual scenes are full of rapid movement, especially those in which the abrupt gestures and furtive glances of the herdsmen join with other visual details to underline the animalism of Karin's attackers. When the victim and her captors are finally seated together in the clearing, the eruptive restlessness of the herdsmen gains emphasis from Karin's ceremonious behavior, first as the goat seizes the girl's flowers, later in the young boy's ravenous interruption of the food blessing, finally in the obscene gurgling of the mute goatherd. Not only the ferocity of the ensuing attack but the texture of this whole sequence thus helps to characterize the violators of Karin's innocence. The last supporting detail is the rageful leaping of the mute, who crushes the church candles the girl has carried with her. With this ensemble of notes, Bergman reduces the viciousness of the murderers to purely animal proportions, which illumines by contrast both Ingeri's malevolent desertion of Karin and Töre's ritualized revenge of her murder.

After this climactic moment, Bergman gives priority to the fire image in order to develop more fully the character of Töre, who becomes the center of dramatic action upon Karin's death. Fire has already been identified with explosive passion, but the early scenes have also hinted at its association with rite. Its ambivalent application to both instinctive and formal behavior now serves to define the hero's ambiguous response to the herdsmen, who prevail upon him for shelter. Ignorant of their crime, he welcomes them into his home, and the fire built to warm them seems to exemplify his sense of patriarchal duty. "Keep the fire burning tonight," he instructs his guest. "It will be bitterly cold." Later, however, the rights of the patriarch will be used to justify taking the lives of the herdsmen. He will murder them, but the violence will be transacted within the context of ritual. Ironically, of course, the ritual proves inadequate to civilize the act, and the fire image underscores his slipping from civility to barbarism. The fire which warms the strangers becomes the fire which steams Töre's body as he cleanses himself for combat, and finally the fire which absorbs almost the entire screen when he strangles one of his antagonists in wild fury.

The ritualistic aspect of Töre's attack upon the herdsmen is also established by the pace of the film in the moments preceding the killing. Extremely well planned, the sequence reveals how completely Bergman realizes the power of photography to fulfill dramatic objectives. At this point dialogue counts for little, tempo and composition for nearly everything. The movement is slow so that suspense may build, so that we may recover from the emotional stress begotten of earlier violence, but also that we may appreciate Töre's resolve to contain his lust for vengeance in some psychically acceptable frame. As the attack of the herdsmen has been completely visceral, so Töre's revenge is fully rationalized. The effect is to point up his sense of responsibility, later important to the understanding of his guilt.

The effectiveness of the fight scene depends heavily upon Bergman's handling of intercut shots. At the outset these are used sparingly, to create a mood of solemn stillness. Even the preparatory activity (felling the birch tree, taking the sauna bath) has proceeded slowly, but movement virtually ceases for several moments after Töre has entered the herdsmen's quarters. The time element seems infinitely long due to the sparseness of intercuts. The isolated sound of the knife striking wood reverberates ominously in the silence. Nothing allows our attention to stray from the protagonist himself, as he assumes his magisterial stance at the seat of honor, then gradually begins to betray nervousness when the helpless captives fail to awaken, and at last searches uneasily for some means to rouse them. On the verge of the encounter, Töre has lost the godlike composure which the camera has studied from multiple angles. As the battle is joined, all differences vanish between hunter and hunted. Frequent intercutting now heightens the fury of combat as Töre's stylized gestures become spasms of animal desperation in his struggle with the second herdsman. Both are seared by the same fire before the avenger overpowers his victim. Ritual has been utterly dissolved in rage.

The film now takes its final dramatic turn, reintroducing the theme of recovery and renewal, while images of running water assume their earlier centrality. As the family sets out to find Karin's body, the original journey is retraced in detail, providing the time interval necessary for Töre to rethink his actions. The penetration of the forest also permits Bergman to repeat earlier landscape shots, but with important omissions. The troll who seemed to preside over the stream Karin had forded no longer intrudes his hideous presence. The water which had gathered in muddy pools now runs in bright rivulets, already suggesting the regeneration of life which the miracle of the spring confirms. Thus anticipated in this rendering of natural landscape, the miraculous rush of water from dry earth becomes a daring but perfectly legitimate extension of images already operative and invested with metaphoric significance. Its upsurge forms an exactly appropriate analogue to the resurgence of vital energy in Töre. Baffled, bereaved, and guilt-ridden, yet willing to tolerate partial perspectives and endure in the face of catastrophe, Bergman's hero reclaims himself as a man at the same moment the nascent stream begins to lift the turf with the force of its life-giving current. Resisting the impulse to sentimentalize and further assimilating the miraculous event into a natural landscape, Bergman closes the film with shots whose background includes the black recesses into which even the sun-drenched waters of the virgin spring must ultimately flow. By this time action and image have received their full aesthetic shape.

CONCLUSION

Looking back from the 1970s, we can now see that these films represent only one phase of Bergman's unfolding career, though—from a formative standpoint—a very important phase. Since about 1960, however, he has been going in a rather different direction. Whereas the films of the fifties were story-centered, Bergman now experiments with more esoteric narrative modes; whereas he used to be genre-conscious (dividing his time between comedies and miracle or morality plays), his films now defy easy categories; and whereas in the fifties he typically made "costume pieces" (almost every film being set at least a generation in the past), his art is now rigorously contemporary and modernist. There has also been a decisive shift of emphasis from masculine to feminine roles. Von Sydow and Björnstrand still figure importantly in Bergman's casting, but they move in what is essentially a woman's world. The allegory of masculine quest in *The Seventh Seal* has been displaced by the introspective feminine explorations of *Persona* (1966); the virile conjuration of *The Magician* has given way to the potent female symbols of divination that control *The Ritual* (1968). Nowhere do we now find the power of von Sydow's Töre from *The Virgin Spring;* maleness seems personified in the helpless dwarfs of *The Silence* (1962) and the floating corpses of *Shame* (1968). The centrality of Liv Ullmann, strong of both body and will, to Bergman's most recent films suitably points up the director's new, and perhaps slightly grudging, homage to the feminine.

As with form and theme, so with style and surface. These too change remarkably as we follow Bergman from the fifties to the sixties. The pace and rhythm of Bergman's pictures has been different since Ulla Ryge took over the cutting room from Rosander and Lennart Wallén in 1961. The transitions are now rougher, deliberately disjunctive, in keeping with the discordant, irresolute tenor of the films themselves. This approach to cutting makes Bergman's films of the sixties look more like early Godard or late Antonioni, less like vintage Dreyer. Composition in the late films differs still more radically, probably reflecting the tastes of Sven Nykvist, who replaced Fischer as head cameraman in 1959. Insisting on "a simplicity which does not disturb," [3] Nykvist has slowly edged Bergman towards greater naturalism in the handling of light. Gone are the glowering skies of the fifties, made picturesque by heavy filtration. Gone too, for the most part, is the low-key, high-contrast spotlighting of *The Seventh Seal* and *Wild Strawberries,* replete with ominous shadows and unexpected flashes. Bergman's late films depend much more upon the glare of sunshine, highlighted only by glints from glass or polished metal, harsh as the austerity of the director's personal psychology. Even when he moves indoors, his films have less the look of the studio. The lighting is diffuse, with few sharp shadows; the decor is spare, rarely invested with obviously symbolic content. The new look in Bergmanian lighting is already implicit in the outdoor world of *The Virgin Spring* (the first film in which Nykvist had full charge of the photography), but the tendency towards naturalism is much more pronounced in *Winter Light, The Silence,* and *Persona.*

Since 1960 Bergman has also conducted his first experiments with color. He used it badly, or at best unimaginatively, in *All These Women* (1963), overburdening the color scheme with obvious allegorical trappings. But *The Passion of Anna* (1970) represents a more flexible application of color, perhaps foreshadowing the Bergman of the 1970s. More noteworthy, however, is the director's new-found fondness for exceptionally long lenses, which is what gives the flat, disklike appearance to the facial portraiture of his recent films. In the 1950s Bergman did most of his close-ups with standard "portrait-length" lenses (85–105 mm. focal length); now his studies of the human face—increasingly more prominent in his pictures—are typically done with telephoto lenses (135–200 mm. focal length) or zoom lenses at their long focal length settings. This achieves what it is fashionable to call the "planarization" of space, in other words, a shallowness of field and a compression of planes that deprives the image of its depth dimension. More than of merely technical significance, this choice of long lenses is optically analogous to the interest in masks and the apparently depthless surfaces of personality which mark Bergman's work of the sixties. For this director, technique is always dramatically functional.

[3] Nykvist, p. 631.

No doubt it is still too soon to speak of Bergman's ultimate stature as a filmmaker. Many complain that he is not a highly original thinker, a charge that to me seems reasonably well grounded. The view that "man lives strictly according to his needs," [4] which he still advertises as the crux of his philosophy, is hardly a startling new insight. Freud said more as much as half a century ago. But to worry over the quality of Bergman's thinking is to confuse the offices of art and philosophy, for Bergman's profundity is engrained in his aesthetic medium. As his camera plays upon the human scene, the textbook abstractions of his thought receive weight and shape, explored as they are in all their nuances and implications, always with a sure sense of the dramatic engagements they engender. Though perhaps conceived in clinical terms, Bergman's characters nearly always take on moral proportions as they accept their biology and aspire to responsible conduct in spite of inherited drives. His sense of man's persistent struggle towards autonomy usually preserves him from triteness.

Throughout his career, Bergman has said pretty much the same thing: man is limited, vulnerable, defensive—yet hungry to learn, both of himself and his world. In the 1950s, after first finding his own voice, Bergman formulated these feelings according to models of reality inherited from a religious past, the personal religious past of his own theological upbringing and the public religious past of Western culture. The usefulness of these models was eventually depleted, at which point he lost interest in crusades and cathedrals and began to look for new emblems of man's permanent condition. Hence his sacramental confessions have become psychoanalytic soliloquies, and his God-sent plagues are now man-sent air raids. In keeping with this new secularism, he has come to depend more upon the private fantasies of his characters and less upon public myths. But what we have in this transition is not so much a change of mind as a change of metaphor. I know of no very good reason to prefer one Bergmanian mode to another, since both periods of his career are distinguished by major achievements. Perhaps the films of the fifties are a little more intellectually accessible, in spite of their dependence upon costume and fable, though we need not argue these questions. It is sufficient to say that in his first creative flourish Bergman gave us several films which have a continuing claim upon our attention. Among these are surely *The Virgin Spring, Wild Strawberries,* and *The Seventh Seal.*

[4] "Bergman Discusses Filmmaking," *Four Screenplays,* p. xxi.

Words and Whisperings:
An Interview with Ingmar Bergman
by BIRGITTA STEENE

In Sweden Bergman's timing in making a film or directing a play is so precise that people can set their clocks and calendars by it. One has the feeling, too, that Bergman faces an interview with the same kind of professional discipline. It is a job to be done and he is going to try his hardest to go through with it. The only thing that might make him withdraw is an interviewer's cough or cold: Bergman is perhaps a bit of a hypochondriac; or perhaps he knows only too well what the flu can do to the schedule of a planned work. (Before starting to shoot a new film, he insists that all personnel take flu shots and gammaglobulin.)

I meet Ingmar Bergman while he is finishing the shooting of *Whisperings and Cries*. The setting is an old estate by Lake Mälar, south of Stockholm. The houses are a bit run down; outside, the park blazons in fall colors. We talk on the carpeted steps between two floors in the main building, where all the rooms have been painted in different shades of red to suggest the symbolic setting of the film: the landscape of the soul—as a child Bergman used to imagine the soul as a damp membrane of red. All around us technicians keep running with lamps and cords, but Bergman shields off the world around him. Once in a while he glances at me, but most of the time he looks straight ahead through his slightly cupped hands, which shadow his face.

How do you react to what is said and written about you?

I never read very carefully what's written about me. All that is *vanitas vanitatum* or whatever it's called. It's as if it concerned someone else, some distant cousin or relative but not myself.

But you still react to what is written about you?

Well, sort of. But very briefly. If someone writes something nasty about me, I fume over it for about half an hour until I get the poison out of my system. If it's something favorable, I probably think about it a little longer, about an hour maybe. But you see, all that must be something very secondary. I simply must discipline myself to ignore all my old films, all my old stage productions and all that is written about me.

So you never think about your old films?

No. To do so would be a terrible burden. I have to weed out all the films I've made in the past. The only thing that matters is what I am doing now and what I plan to do. The rest is irrelevant.

Does that mean that you don't like your old films?

Some I like more and some less. But I don't think about them.

So you never think about The Seventh Seal *for instance?*

No.

But you do like that film?

Birgitta!!!

I know. But the film is terribly important to some of us. I know the impact of the film when I show it to my students.

It makes me happy to hear that. But it's irrelevant. The only thing that matters is what I am doing now and what I plan to do. And right now I'm making *Whisperings and Cries.*

And what do you plan to do?

I don't know. But when I'm making a film, my mind works at top speed. Often new ideas come to my mind and out of these a new film might be born.

Do you ever change a film while you're shooting it?

I didn't use to. But now it varies. *The Touch* changed character while we made it. *Persona* was a film that evolved as we worked with it.

Your manuscripts look different today, don't they?

Yes, they are much less complete. When I wrote something like *The Seventh Seal,* there was a frustrated dramatist in me. I wrote stage plays for the screen in those days, because the theater seemed closed to me. But nowadays I don't work that way anymore.

The verbal aspect of your films has also changed.

Yes! God, those old films with their stilted literary language!

It seems to me that when you begin to move away from a literary language, you begin to use more close-ups.

I don't think so. I think that's critical rationalization. I've always believed in the close-up. In the close-up lies the great suggestive power of the film medium.

Did you become more aware of the close-up after the breakthrough of television in Sweden in the early sixties?

No, not at all. I've always used the close-up. You can look at any of my old films and you'll see that it's true. But of course it's easier today. It was darn tricky in the old days to make close-ups. But because the camera lenses are more sensitive today and the raw film is faster and the lighting technique simpler and the personnel handling the camera more capable, we can use more close-ups. Then, too, you must remember that in the old days the producer cried like a pig when we used close-ups. No, for god's sake, he used to say, we don't want a meat market on the screen!

You don't think the close-up can be overused? I am often irritated by the habit of television cameras to select a small detail of the face, the mouth for instance.

Yes, but then you're not talking about close-ups anymore. You're talking about detailed shots. And those can often be very suspect. But with a close-up I mean a shot of the face that includes the mouth and the eyes. A close-up is created by the expression around a person's mouth and by the angle of his eyes and the skin around the eyes.

Do words seem important to you at all today?

Words are used to conceal reality, aren't they? I'm not very good at words. When I try to say something in words, I always seem to lose half of what I want to communicate.

So that's why you use music instead to convey rapport between people?

Yes. Music is a much more reliable means of communication.

But you still use words in your latest films?

Yes. *The Silence* and *Persona* were experiments. Attempts to see how far I could go without words. But now image and dialogue—as well as other sound—seem more like equal units; in the tension between image and word a new dimension is created.

You said that you feel you lose half of what you want to say when you use words. But you talk with a great deal of ease.

Yes, but you know, I've had to train myself to become articulate with words. In fact, my whole intellectual capacity is a matter of training, of self-discipline. You see, I've always had a hard time learning to reason logically. Anything that doesn't have an emotional anchoring is practically incomprehensible to me. In school, for instance, I was totally, completely devoid of any talent for math. Even today I can hardly add two and two. To subtract is even more difficult for me, not to speak of division or the multiplication table. In school, geography was also a difficult subject.

Was it too abstract?

Yes. All those maps. But history was a great deal of fun. And religion. All those stories in the Old Testament. Latin was fun too.

That seems strange to me.

No, that's not so strange. Because to study Latin was a combination of detective work and a kind of intuition. It was terribly exciting to figure out those old texts.

So you didn't study Latin the mechanical way Minus does in Through a Glass Darkly?

Bergman's answer is his famous big, hearty laugh.

·◦⧼ REVIEWS ⧽◦·

JURGEN SCHILDT

❖❖

Certain critical voices have mingled with the praises that the comedies of Ingmar Bergman have received in recent years, voices oscillating between bewilderment and disappointment, questioning if comedy actually was Mr. Bergman's home territory. His work was brilliant (most often), it was witty (sometimes), it was formally perfect (almost always), but—so the voices went—where did the sting go, the bite into so-called essential matters, the ethical content without which the aesthetic remains a skin without a core? Had Bergman accepted for good the role of bourgeois jester, had he become an Oscar Wilde in the welfare state of the fifties, or did he have more important tools up his sleeve?

He did. With his own play *Wood Painting* in one hand and Dr. Dymling in the other he began the retreat of the comedian, perhaps a temporary one but nevertheless glorious. In the interest of optimistic history writing, let us not be misled to see this as the beginning of a new era in Mr. Bergman's professional toiling; even he can fall for what he calls, in the program note, "the relatively legitimate professional temptation of seeing himself and his family adequately provided for." Let us instead, if only for a day and a moment, establish that *The Seventh Seal* is a film in the great international class, a remarkable work, accomplished with the willfulness that often is the banner of genius.

Strictly speaking, we had expected Bergman to tackle a medieval motif sooner or later. His world is, like that of the medieval morality plays, a world in black and white, a battlefield between good and evil, between Satan and—no—not God but Something Else. For Bergman hesitates before the final step; as a religious type he is more of a believing skeptic. Apart from that, most aspects of the

From Veckojournalen, *no. 9 (1957).* © *1957 by Vecko-Journalen. Reprinted by permission of International Magazine Service. Translated from the Swedish by Birgitta Steene.*

story mark the fact that it is really a question of two irreconcilable worlds. There is light and space around the figure of the knight—his men on the chess set are white. Death plays with black pieces —his hood and cape are black, his background is dark as the night and makes his face appear a plastered mask in the void. The chess game is the old game about Everyman.

But what is the central action and, more important than that, what is the ethical and spiritual meaning? The film is not easy to get at, hence any attempt at an interpretation runs the risk of becoming lies and half-truths. The main character is, it seems, the knight Antonius Block, returning with his squire from the Crusades. Somewhere on the coast in the plague-threatened Sweden of the 1350s he meets Death, who has come to demand his tribute. The knight and Death play chess about life, with the result that the knight gets a brief respite. He wants to use the deferment to do "one single meaningful act" in an existence pierced with metaphysical question marks.

Here the dark thread is crossed by a light one. The knight meets the juggler Jof and his wife Mia (read: Joseph and Mary)—two big children who, in a plague-ridden world, take time to prattle in the green grass, take time to be irresponsible, to believe in life-as-play. Their simple wisdom could have been hung as a wall hanging in the wagon: "It is always better when one is two." But Death also cuts across their path. It is now that the knight gets his chance to do his Messiah act, his "one single meaningful act." In the second and decisive move he is in a winning position. But realizing that the choice is between him or Jof's family, he topples his chess pieces, loses the game, and thereby saves the life of his companions: a play about goodness and death.

It is unusual that a Swedish film hits the big tone as often as Bergman does in this medieval drama. The entrance of the flagellants in the pest-ridden village; the first meeting between the knight and Death on the shore with the cold, grey horizon as a background; the procession of the doomed ones across the heath, commanded by Death: again and again one comes across masterpieces of a harsh, naked, almost ascetic visual style. The subject gives the form; how far away are we not from the kind of stylization used by Carné in his medieval legend *Children of the Night*. The name of the photographer is guarantee enough and he is, as most often in Bergman, Gunnar Fischer.

One reservation concerns the role of the squire, the way it has been entrusted to Gunnar Björnstrand. It is he who is mostly responsible for comic passages in the film. Granted that he calls the sighing of the Beasts "this damned apocalyptic chatter"; maybe Bergman needs such modern slang to create a distance to his own seriousness. But add to this Mr. Björnstrand's Stockholm lingo, highly effective but pulverized and skitlike, and the effect is a fatal anachronism. Fifties are fifties, but there are still 600 years in between [1350–1950].

From the point of view of performance, the film is above all Max von Sydow's. His knight does not seem to be chasing just any little truth, but the Holy Grail. His face is young and yet worn; his fever and his worry, his craving for the absolute cuts right through his dense interpretation. As Death Bengt Ekerot gives, if my memory is right, his finest contribution to the cinema, and the overall acting is also on a safe level, including Bibi Andersson who undoubtedly is very talented and Nils Poppe who in the part as Jof at long last gets a well-deserved role.

"And when he had opened the seventh seal, there was silence in heaven about the space of half an hour." And when Ingmar Bergman broke *The Seventh Seal* there was in the theater a silence that lasted about an hour and a half. It could be bewilderment that kept the audience silent. But it is more likely to have been a feeling of intense emotion.

HANSERIK HJERTÉN

❖❖

When leaving Ingmar Bergman's new film *The Seventh Seal*, one is depressed and brooding. One remembers the artistic photography

From Dagstidningen, *February 19, 1957. Reprinted by permission of the author. Translated from the Swedish by Birgitta Steene.*

of Gunnar Fischer, the superior performance of Gunnar Björnstrand, and the novel pleasure of seeing Max von Sydow. But apart
from that, everything is a failure. And one feels sorry for the director, who apparently has wished to return to the tragic genre
after his last few years of mishmash; and one must ask why it is
that one is so untouched.

The casting is one reason, of course. The deficient result seems to
depend on equal parts of routine in the choice of actors, their in-
competence, and their lack of direction. Thus one gets to see Nils
Poppe as a fragment of Soldier Bom [a kind of Swedish Soldier
Schweik], quite insensitive to the demands of the jester's role, help-
lessly left to his empty grin by the director. Here Inga Gill appears
like some medieval version of a Stockholm broad and does not come
off any better because she is dressed up in a ballad. Here Bibi
Andersson gets to reveal, in a major role, all her apprentice im-
maturity. Etc.

But the worst error lies, of course, in the script. Bergman has
wanted to create a drama full of questions about death and the
meaning of life, about God's existence and man's nausea at himself.
He has set it all up like some kind of Judgment Day on earth. Last
Saturday he said on the radio that he saw a parallel to our time,
between the Middle Ages and the age of the hydrogen bomb. It is
a stimulating idea but the film falls flatly to the ground. Why?

I cannot see any other explanation but that Bergman has made
a horror film for children instead of a mature exposé and that he
himself has functioned like a frightened child. He has rumbled on
with all the apocalyptic visions that belong to naive nightmares.
When Anders Ek stands there in a monk's hood, screaming about
death for all that he is worth, it is as if one hears the film's own
voice. A mood of catastrophe is not emphasized by this confused
exhibitionism, quite the contrary.

Here someone might object that it belongs to the milieu that
Bergman has chosen for his allegory. The Middle Ages appear to
us as a stylized dance of death. All simple horror effects gain acceptance in this world. At this point one begins actually to think
about Smiles of a Summer Night, for there is a formal relationship
between the two films which is interesting.

Bergman chose the form of parody for Smiles of a Summer Night,
and most critics saw in this a perfect alibi for all the horrid stupidity
that was being served, as if "parody" were a magic word that made

all criticism stop functioning. It is much the same with *The Seventh Seal*. If you cut out the core, it turns out to be very reminiscent of the puerile quality of the films of the forties. The knight's squire says about the Crusade that it was so terrible only an idealist could have thought it up. Does Bergman have in mind these old films? If so, this "wood painting" in the spirit of Dürer and Albertus Pictor has not helped him out of the dilemma. Bergman appears more and more as his own imitator.

But apart from that one thinks most immediately of *The Road to Heaven* and sees also most clearly what Bergman is lacking: a firm anchoring in the milieu and a clear conception of what he wants to say. His pronouncements in the program are a kind of tossing of words that don't make him liable to anything. This vacillation fits right in with *The Seventh Seal* and with Ingmar Bergman's whole artistic situation.

It may sound blasphemous to many ears, but after this film one would like to suggest that Bergman stop filming for a while. Otherwise economic and artistic failures may force him to do so, which would be worse. Perhaps he could come back later and do justice to his burning desire to create.

JEAN MAMBRINO

❖❖❖

The most bounteous and the most unadorned work, the most complex and the most transparent, all illuminated by the exuberance of language and yet suffused by a severe silence.

When I received the telegram from one of the triumvirs of the Editorial Staff, asking me to write, within three days, a review of

From Cahiers du Cinéma *14, no. 83 (May 1958):43–46. Reprinted by permission of Éditions de l'Étoile and Grove Press, Inc. Translated from the French by Marie Georgette Steisel.*

The Seventh Seal, I almost answered him, just as during the golden age of surrealism: "Poetry not dead. Article follows."

Never did a film demonstrate better, indeed, the soundness of Kafka's words: "The strings of the lyre of modern poets are immense reels of celluloid." *The Seventh Seal* is nothing but poetry, the most beautiful poetry which has ever shone on a screen, and that is the reason for its intricate simplicity. There are no ideas here, no theses, no hidden motives, no hidden scheme, no answer prepared in advance, nothing that might allow classification of this work into reassuring categories, nor is there any license to use it as a controversial weapon. A flawless poem, terrible and beautiful. ("Beauty is always tragic," Bloy used to say, "for it is the song of a deprivation.")

But, since we must summarize the subject, let us not conceal our pleasure in letting the author himself carry out this duty: "In my film, the Crusader returns from the Crusades, as the soldier returns from the war today. In the Middle Ages men lived in terror of the plague. Today they live in fear of the atomic bomb. *The Seventh Seal* is an allegory with a theme that is quite simple: man, his eternal search for God, with death as his only certainty." I'll concede the allegory, and, for those who want to "know the story," let us dwell a little longer on the commentary: this knight in the midst of the ravaging plague represents man in search of an answer to his destiny; his squire rides by his side, as the representative of the bawdiest free-thinking; there are a presumed witch burnt alive, a renegade priest, horrible flagellating monks, and finally, a charming family of jugglers emanating the joy of living, unconcern, and purity. They alone shall manage to go without mishap through the human forest whose trunks fall over, one after the other, in the wake of Death.

Once this summary is over, everything has been said, and nothing has been said.

But here the demanding spectator will, perhaps, raise a few objections. To the extent that Ingmar Bergman (a puritan-born agnostic) claims to evoke the Middle Ages, it is impossible to be satisfied. Then men were living in fear of the plague, but just as much in hope of life, an eternal and inexhaustible life. Their joy was as vast and white as the cathedrals, those mirrors of the world, where human beings, demons, angels, and saints are swarming in a sylvan

setting of leaves and magic animals with a bleeding tree directing
the mad ronde. And the entire immense vessels, facing eastward,
sing in the rising sunlight. There is the true medieval era, an era
of wisdom, of earthiness; in no way hallucinated, despite all appearances. As learned as it is naive, as refined as it is brutal, at the same
time scoffing and adoring, open to all human and divine adven-
tures. Certainly death was feared, but not in terms of life: in terms
of salvation, thus giving to existence a tragic depth, although never
a desperate one, for mercy won over all in spite of all the crimes.
"All shall be well, and all matter of things shall be well," untiringly
declared Julienne de Norwich, the sixteenth-century illiterate mystic,
at the end of her visions.

In passing, let us make clear a point of exegesis: the part of the
Apocalypse which inspired the author, in its true context, has no
connection with death. It deals with an old biblical theme: that of
the Universal Judgment, the "Day of Reckoning" which catastro-
phes and wars throughout history proclaim, without special emphasis on individual death. Thus, in the Holy Scriptures, the seventh
seal, as it opens, does not disclose the secrets of life and death, but
the Last Judgment of all mankind. And it is by the Lamb that it is
broken. The entire Apocalypse is nothing but a song of consolation
and hope: "And God himself shall be with them, and be their God.
And God shall wipe away all tears from their eyes; and there shall
be no more death." This mood is absent from Bergman's production.

At this point one must go back to the film to discover how much
it transcends the [author's] summary. It is not a contrived allegory,
it is "a thought conceived during one's youth and realized at a
ripe old age." Bergman confesses that the idea came out of his
childhood reveries, precisely when during the Sunday sermons he
would look with equal joy and fear at the fabulous universe of
medieval sculptures, the angels, the beasts, the demons, the saints
whirling around in a background of light and shadow. And, under
the cross, a knight would play chess with Death, an admirable
image, which allows the poem to be revealed at its source. Then
the characters loom up in front of us from the depths of unsullied
eyes; they do not want to "say" anything, nor prove anything, they
have several possible meanings, for the author confesses that "many
years ago belief and doubt became—and still are—his faithful companions." Thus he has not changed drastically, he is still pursuing

all the same dreams, all of his childhood terrors, all of his desires. The squire makes jokes, becomes indignant, helps the innocent. The knight looks around, prays, and begs. The crowd sprawls about, or scourges itself. Jugglers dance and smile and children play. And Death, a prodigious face of living wax where only the eyes are flaming black, lurks at every corner with his chess game, and he too is ignorant of the final secret. But at the end of the road, when the frightful storm closes on the group gathered inside the old castle, it is a little maidservant, mute up to that moment, who with a humble smile, faces the Inexorable and pronounces the words of Christ: "It is finished."

Being so frail and so threatened, life does appear even more beautiful, and, from all of nature in Bergman's creation radiates a dazzling and pale light, a light which in itself is a premonition. Nothing matches these great silver skies, only the darkish-whitish sea that proclaims from the very beginning the advent of Death, and from then on accompanies him in a disconsolate lamentation. We breathe in the stinging wind on the beach, or in the aroma of leaves on the meadows at dawn. And each face is imprinted on the tender screen of the world, with the weight of its flesh, the texture of its skin, the furrows of its tears, of its smiles. To be sure the mark of death is already piercing under the most rugged or the most delicate of facial features, but it seems that at times death itself is nothing but the mask of still another face. Here there is nothing but looking and questioning. Righteous and passionate looks exchanged by the living: they seek each other, flee each other, caress and inflame each other. Insistent yet mute looks exchanged between the living and Death. Long dialogues against a silent background, which are born out of silence and return to silence, like a song that rises from the depths of man, an echo which would reverberate inside each one of us during the hour which separates dawn from night.

Each frame unites darkness and light according to an almost magic dosage, and it would be well-nigh impossible to determine their fine dividing line. Both solid and fluid frames perpetually dissolve under our very eyes, in motionless movements. One senses here Bergman's theatrical background, yet the hierarchy of the scenes, the plastic composition of the imagery, possess the fascinating charm of pictures born of the vapor of dreams. Not one omission: everything is shown; but all begins beyond words and symbols, a hidden splendor is revealed as it is being erased. Here, for the first time in the movies, is the forbidding sun of "El Desdichado," and I muse at the last sentence of the note written by Gerard de Nerval a few hours before he plunged into Paris to die: "In a short while the night will be black and white. . . ."

DILYS POWELL

Few would deny that *The Seventh Seal* . . . provides a pretty sobering occasion. Certainly its director, Ingmar Bergman, meant it to be sobering. He meant it, in spite of its medieval setting, to frighten you and me about here and now. In fact, it has what, for want of a couple of longer words, I will call contemporary application.

The Seventh Seal takes its title from Revelation, its opening words from the chapter which, beginning "And when he had opened the seventh seal, there was silence in heaven about the space of half an hour," announces universal destruction; the sea turned to blood, the star Wormwood falling, "burning as it were a lamp." The film is an allegory, but an allegory much of which is in realistic terms; when Mr. Bergman cries Woe he intends not some vague alarm but physical agony before your eyes.

And he has set his story in a period when there seems, at any rate to those of us who are not devoted medievalists, to have been a pretty general addiction to agony. A knight and his squire come back to Sweden from the Crusades. They find their world changed. The Black Death rages: corpses on the seashore, in the farmyard, in the forest. There is a frenzy to avert the anger of heaven; flagellants drag themselves whining through the villages, witches are blamed for the plague, tortured, and burned. The knight himself has altered in ten years of fighting and wandering. He is no longer

From The London Sunday Times, *March 9, 1958. Reprinted by permission of* The London Sunday Times.

certain of anything: he broods, he doubts, he questions. Over everything there hangs the menace of some still huger, some final disaster.

To hobble Saint John the Divine as a handy guide to a modern
situation is not as new as some appear to think; one recalls without
indulgence how a lot of well-meaning people wore out, by applying
it to the conflict of 1914–18, the word Armageddon. But I must not
suggest that Mr. Bergman is merely battening on the Book of Revelation. What he has done is, drawing on the figures of medieval
religious painting—Death, the Holy Family, the Crusader—and
using a mixture of historical imagination and, as I say, allegory, to
make a film about fear of the H-bomb.

The soldier back from the wars, loss of belief, pervasive fright—
the analogy is clear enough. And it is splendidly illustrated. Most
of those who are accustomed to looking with attention at the cinema
will admit the force of the images of cruelty, squalor, and beast-
liness. And they will recognise the quality of the facial types, seeing
in the exhausted, Gothic lantern head of the knight (Max von
Sydow) the gnawing disquiet of the unsatisfied agnostic, in the
stubborn, sardonic grimace of the squire (a fine performance by
Gunnar Björnstrand, and the only *character* in the film; the rest
are wall-paintings) the endurance of the honest materialist. *The
Seventh Seal* is a notable film, let me make no bones about that;
and since notable films are rare we were happy as well as lucky to
be able, in the London Film Festival last October, to give it a first
showing in London.

And now, the honors done, perhaps I may be allowed to add that
I find it repulsive.

When I first saw the film I thought my nausea was a simple reaction from the emphasis on the deformed and the tortured: the
crippled flagellants, the young witch howling as, waiting for execution, she comes back to consciousness (whenever the Scandinavian
cinema has five minutes to fill in it burns a witch). It is an emphasis
in which from the start I saw not the pain of the sensitive artist
forcing himself to record a hateful truth but the watchfulness of
the inquisitor. But now that I know *The Seventh Seal* better I find
my revulsion going much farther. The magnificent craftsmanship, of
course, I admit. But beneath the surface of the high-class, bony
morality which has understandably attracted so much admiration
there lurks what to me is a dreadful squashy sentimentality, the

kind of sentimentality which goes hand in hand with obsession by the dark and the cruel. On the one side the executioners and the hysterical self-indulgers, on the other the naive dreamer, the loving fair-haired wife in a low-necked blouse, the chubby baby. And it goes almost without saying that the dreamer is a strolling player. Innocence in the circus tent and the caravan: it is the oldest hat in the business.

Death playing chess on the seashore—it would be consoling to be able to say that the magniloquent symbols conceal something bogus as well as sentimental. But they don't; Mr. Bergman, I am sure, has a midnight, Arctic-winter sincerity; the violence of my dislike of his film is probably evidence of that. Did I say *The Seventh Seal* was sobering? On me it has the impact of one of those spiked iron balls chained to a club, so popular in films about good-will in the Middle Ages.

PETER JOHN DYER

❖◈◈◈❖

The Seventh Seal . . . is a revelation, both in its authentic strangeness and in the new light it throws upon its director, Ingmar Bergman. With this extraordinary film one can discard previous reservations—Bergman is a craftsman with a real vision, working within a commercial establishment, for whom filmmaking is and can be nothing less than a personal catharsis. Buñuel, Mizoguchi, Fellini, and (so far as we know) Vajda—these are among the cinema's visionaries, men such as Granach's strolling juggler in *Warning Shadows,* who reveal the truth through hallucinations, the truth that is their own truth or no truth at all. At one time it seemed doubtful whether Bergman was of this company. Admittedly both *Sawdust and Tinsel,* a painful, twisted study in humiliation, and *Smiles of a Summer Night,* a frosted, bittersweet exercise in *fin-de-*

From Sight and Sound 27, no. 4 (Spring 1958):199–200. Reprinted by permission of the author and Sight and Sound.

siècle romanticism, showed the highly individual expertise of the conjuror. Youth, age, love, and death prowled the dark corridors; hidden tensions hovered on the brink of a private myth. But was it not all a shade too rococo, too calculated, a series of graceful and mannered distractions? And did not these distractions cover up a certain constraint verging on solipsism? It is the easiest and most fatal thing in the world for a director, the vitality of whose work springs from an intense, revolutionary urge towards self-expression, to find himself imprisoned by his own *alter ego*. This is a problem Fellini still has to face; and one that Bergman, in *The Seventh Seal,* has faced and overcome with assurance.

In the first place, he is a born storyteller. His title is taken from the Apocalypse, and his story—set in fourteenth-century Sweden— begins and ends with a powerful sense of omen and wonder. A bird hovers and screams, the seashore is beaten by breakers, two horses taste and smell the ocean, a squire (Gunnar Björnstrand), returned from the Crusades, lies exhausted on the sand, and his knight (Max von Sydow) challenges Death to a hopeless, delaying game of chess. While the phantasmal contest is in progress, knight and squire journey across the plague-stricken countryside. The knight, tormented by doubts about the existence of God, finds momentary peace as he eats and drinks with a little family of strolling players. The squire, a tough, carnal, reassuringly eupeptic cynic, saves a girl from a corpse-robber and prays that his wife is by now dead. As they proceed, they encounter a group of howling, hysterical flagellants; a mad girl is burnt as a witch; an old ham actor who plays the part of Death steals the blacksmith's wife, fakes suicide to escape the blacksmith, then relaxes in the bough of a tree, congratulating himself on his latest performance, only to find Death sawing down his refuge. The chess game is all but over, and still the knight has failed to give meaning to his life by one last gesture of faith in his fellow men. He finally cheats Death of his fullest hopes by upsetting the chessboard—a momentary distraction that allows the chosen innocents, the strolling player, his wife and child, to escape. But the rest of the company must face their destiny. Death comes to them in the knight's castle and goads them, hand-in-hand like a troupe of solemn dancing clowns, silhouetted against the stormy skyline, over the horizon of the distant hill "toward the dark lands. . . ."

This is a wholly indigenous film, with something of Stiller's sophistication and Sjöström's sense of elemental worship—indigenous, that is, in its style. It is also a mature embodiment of child-

hood's nightmare fears, still to be seen in all their perverted horror
painted on the walls of those medieval country churches where
Bergman's father once performed funerals and baptisms and
preached sermons. It is a period film in the sense that *Ugetsu
Monogatari* is a period film, but not in any way in the manner of
Fritz Lang's *Destiny*, where an almost identical subject was handled
with heady, heavy, defeated romanticism. There is no implied retreat or pessimism in Bergman's choice of subject, even though his
main images are familiar from any number of medieval morality
plays and Chaucerian comedies. These archetypal symbols have
been appropriated to lend the film clarity in its quality of time-
lessness and also its contemporary relevance. The witch-hunters, the
penitents, and the pillagers are still among us; we are each of us of
their breed, deaf, denying, stifled by insecurity, while a bird hovers
and screams its warning above—an omen of the age of the H-bomb.

Death answers nothing. He remains a dispassionate, cultured, soft-
mannered old gentleman, treading softly through a lonely world.
Cowled and black-robed, Bengt Ekerot, in perhaps the best performance of a wonderfully well-acted film, makes him a macabre
though never bizarre figure. In the film, questions are asked, facts
accepted; the innocent and artist (the strolling player) sees visions
and the future is his. Bergman answers what he can, though of
course there remain mysteries in his film, locked doors over which
he keeps jealous watch; and part of the quality of his film lies in
what is not explained, in its obscure tensions and unsolved problems.

COLIN YOUNG

◆◆◆

The Seventh Seal, the latest of Swedish director Ingmar Bergman's recent films to reach this country, is a triumphant declaration

From Film Quarterly *12, no. 3 (Spring 1959):42–44.* © *1959 by The
Regents of the University of California. Reprinted by permission of
the author and the Regents.*

of what is occasionally and uniquely possible in the cinema—*occasionally*, since . . . a personal commitment in film is rarely possible, and *uniquely*, since Bergman demonstrates a control over and synthesis of narrative, performance, and style which are uniquely available in the cinema, and then only to its masters.

The film is set in fourteenth-century Sweden, at the height of the Black Plague. Disease, pestilence, fear are everywhere. Women give birth to monsters—children with the heads of calves—and death may at any time, and for anybody, overtake life. A young woman is suspected of being intimate with the Devil, and is to be burned as a witch. Priests drag gigantic crosses and lead supplicants through the streets, lashing each other with thonged whips in a desperate attempt to pacify the "God who lives forever." A church muralist, with the relish of a man who knows he is doomed, records these events so that future congregations will be properly impressed and frightened.

It is into this gloomy but dramatically rich situation that Bergman places his leading characters—principally a knight and his squire, returned to Sweden after ten years at the Crusades, disillusioned. The knight is now engaged in a double quest—to perform some one significant act, and to discover, if he can, the meaning of life. To provide a form for this potentially unruly content, a limit is placed on the knight's time. As the film opens (after an astonishingly evocative shot of a large-winged bird hovering in the empty sky) the knight is found resting on a rocky beach. It is dawn. Close to the knight is his squire, asleep. And beside him lies, open and prepared, an ornate chess set. Suddenly the sound of the sea and of the wind is cut; the knight looks up and finds himself confronted with Death. In order to buy the time that he needs for his quest, he challenges Death to a game of chess. The game continues at intervals throughout the film, and although the issue is never in doubt it provides the film with a constant reference point and the setting for a running relationship between Death and the knight. The knight is plagued, not so much by the prospect of death, as with the knowledge that he can neither kill God within him nor find a belief that God exists, either now or in an afterlife. The present life, filled with suffering and despair and inhumanity, would have no meaning—only nausea and disgust—if there were no prospect of deliverance. Thus death has to be a transition to something else—to an afterlife which will explain and justify the present. His squire, with whom he has a continuing argument, and who is silenced (under protest) only by death itself, is much more of a rationalist. Less idealistic, with a hedonist's relish of life, he knows death only as an end to life, and as such it has to be resisted.

These two attitudes are most completely contrasted during a brilliantly staged scene—the burning of the witch. The knight, willing to go anywhere for knowledge, asks the girl for her secrets, but her replies are enigmatic, almost flippant. She is tied to a ladder and raised above the pyre. The knight sees hope in her eyes, the squire only the despair of someone looking at a void. And then, significantly, she dies on the ladder. She has been saved from the executioners, but the knight's questions have not been answered.

In the end Death also is a disappointment. At the moment of his triumph over the knight he is silent, and declares that in fact he has no secrets. Thus the argument between the knight and his squire goes unresolved, and if the film ended here we would be left with a sense of despair and, almost, of personal loss.

However, woven into this central engagement are a number of other characters whose lives and attitudes are made to bear upon the knight's quest. There is a group of strolling players, whose director, Skat, seduces the wife of a blacksmith and, to escape his wrath, feigns suicide. Resting in the bough of a tree from the exertion of what might have been his most important performance, he is startled to find that Death is sawing down his refuge. The blacksmith and his wife, representatives of common-sense self-indulgence, continue, awed for a moment (ironically, by the false death) but, to all intents and purposes, not seriously involved. Death will be a shock when it comes to them, but that's all. The remaining members of his band remind us of the holy family, and their names are the same, save that the child is called, not Jesus, but after the archangel Michael. Resting with this family in the bright sun of a Swedish summer afternoon, and eating wild strawberries with them, the knight has a temporary respite from doubt. Later, just after Death has captured his queen, he is given the chance to save their lives. Aware that Mary's life has been called, the knight upsets the board and temporarily distracts Death, so that Mary and Joseph, with their child, are able to make their escape. Thus, although failing in his larger quest, the knight performs a solitary significant act, and has a minor triumph over Death. And here, probably, is the substance of Bergman's argument. Both the knight and the squire are, by their philosophical positions, unable to dispatch the problems presented by death, but Mary and Joseph never commit themselves to this argument and are, in fact, aloof from it and from the double scourge of pestilence and a reactionary church. Calm and serene, they are the only ones who in the end are saved.

Death comes as a relief only to a woman whose life earlier had been saved by the squire, who hoped to make her his housekeeper (hoping also that in the meantime his wife has died). She kneels before Death and says—with her only line of dialogue throughout the film, and with as close as she ever gets to a smile—"It is finished." "Consummatum est"—the last words of Christ on the cross. The Apocalypse is at hand.

The various internal dramas of the film are brilliantly controlled by Bergman. His skill in staging a scene, in composing it, in moving the camera, and in obtaining performances of stature from a varied cast is breathtaking. He owes much to his cameraman, Gunnar Fischer, who also photographed *Smiles of a Summer Night* and several other Bergman films, and it is only in minor places that Bergman might be thought to falter, although the choice of music (by Erik Nordgren) seems oddly theatrical. Perhaps his principal dramatic achievement, in the script as much as in the direction, is to leave us with a feeling always of character, never only of symbol. In a piece which is nonetheless rich in symbolic imagery, the characters emerge as people. Twice when we might otherwise question the real humanity of the knight, Bergman introduces the character of his wife, first by allusion and then, near the end, in person. The knight is humanized and made more significant by this personal extension and also by his relationship with the squire. Both of these parts are brilliantly played—the squire with a kind of well-mannered and articulate sensuality by Gunnar Björnstrand, and the knight by Max von Sydow, tortured, twisted with doubt, but always a knight, always with the authority and integrity of his position. Bengt Ekerot, as Death, avoids most of the medieval clichés and, although of course deprived of the opportunity for a personal relationship with any of the characters, is still not impersonal; not only a symbol, but a character who is capable also of personal doubt.

The film is a successful period piece in the sense that it creates the precise period and locale which permit the story and the characters to develop. But the references to contemporary times, the age of anxiety and of the atom bomb, are not hard to find. The title, and some of the narrative, is taken from the Revelation of

St. John the Divine (chapters five through nine), but the allusions, in dialogue and in song, owe as much to Nordic mythology as to any Biblical origin. The film, made through Svensk Filmindustri, is an extraordinary major studio production—a remarkable, personal work, which establishes Bergman (for those who had any doubt) as the leading European director.

HENRY HART

◆◇◆

Ingmar Bergman, who has just turned forty, is Sweden's most interesting contemporary director.

He began his career as a producer of amateur theatricals, became an assistant producer at the Stockholm Opera, now writes and directs films, and is advisor to several theaters in the Swedish provinces. He directed *Smiles of a Summer Night* and wrote, but did not direct, 1944s *Torment*.

His father is a well-known Stockholm clergyman and Bergman says that as a child he accompanied his father to the small country churches in which his father preached. During the sermon he puzzled over the paintings and carved figures which had been in the churches from medieval times.

"There was everything that one's imagination could desire," says Bergman, "angels, saints, dragons, prophets, devils, humans. There were very frightening animals: serpents in paradise, Balaam's ass, Jonah's whale, the eagle of Revelation. All this was surrounded by heavenly, earthly, and subterranean landscapes of strange yet familiar beauty. In a wood sat Death, playing chess with a Crusader. Clutching the branch of a tree was a naked man with staring eyes, while down below stood Death, sawing away to his heart's content.

From Films in Review *9 (November 1958):516–17. Reprinted by permission of the author.*

Across gentle hills Death led the final dance towards the dark lands."

The ideas symbolized in such medieval imagery were beyond the boy's comprehension, but the symbols remained, as symbols will, in his psyche, and their meanings emerged as he matured. Finally, after he had become proficient in the art of the motion picture, Bergman resolved to depict the "current dilemmas" of man via these old symbols. The major dilemmas: man's lack of belief that existence has meaning, and man's fear of something ghastlier than anything in the Book of Revelation—the hydrogen bomb.

The script Bergman wrote for the film he calls *The Seventh Seal* and also directed, can be synopsized as follows:

> A mid-fourteenth-century Swedish knight, returning home disillusioned from a Crusade, doubts the existence of God and the worth of life. Nevertheless, when he and his squire encounter Death, he is not willing to die, and proposes that Death play him a game of chess and that he be allowed to live until the game is finished. The knight and his squire then encounter some of the horrible effects of a plague that has ravaged Sweden. They also come upon a little family of strolling players who, in the midst of desolation and evil, have kept their joy in life, whereupon the knight enables this little family to elude Death.

The foregoing, considered as a framework for a motion picture, is treacherous material. Death is difficult to personify believably, and the knight, his squire, the strolling players, and the other characters deployed here are not true symbols. That is to say, what they symbolize is not universally recognizable.

As for the actions of these imperfectly symbolical characters, Bergman involves them in incidents about which he has not thought deeply. The result: eschatological things are treated in a kind of impromptu vaudeville, some of it irrelevant, and some of it macabre.

The dialogue, even allowing for possible ineptitude by the English subtitler, is often pretentiously cryptic. For example: "My heart is a void in which I see my face." "We make an idol of [our] fear and call it God." "The Crusade was so stupid only an idealist could have thought it up." "To believe is to suffer—like loving someone in the dark who does not respond." "I see terror—nothing else." "We feel something will happen to us but we don't know what."

The Seventh Seal was made very inexpensively, and its inadequate sets and costumes do not provide visualizations and intimations of medieval times. Its cast is capable, but not always effective. Max von Sydow, as the knight, looked too much like a blondined dead-pan in the avant-garde films made by sex perverts. Gunnar Björn-strand, however, played the squire with vitality and insight. Bengt Ekerot, as Death, merely wore a black cape and hood and a face full of rice powder. But Bibi Andersson, as the girl-wife of a strolling player, was both a pleasing personality and a versatile actress. As her husband, Nils Poppe, Sweden's most popular comedian, gave the best performance. Now almost fifty, he seemed much younger. The excellent black-and-white photography of Gunnar Fischer fre-quently obscured the inadequacy of the sets and costumes.

Despite its defects, *The Seventh Seal* will interest all who are interested in the mystery of man's existence. It would have inter-ested everybody had Bergman pondered his script longer—for as long, say, as Goethe pondered *Faust*.

THEO FÜRSTENAU

◆◇◆

A horrible vision staggers, groaning and ghostlike, across the screen. People moan under the crucifix on which is nailed the emaciated, ecstatically twisted body of Christ. With insane eyes and monotonous uniformity they hit their harassed bodies with the scourge. This procession of the plague, this picture of despair, of nonsalvation, of blind faith caused by confusion seems like an agonizing, self-paralyzing pantomime of horror.

"Apocalypse und Todentantz" by *Theo Fürstenau. From* Die Zeit *(Hamburg), February 16, 1962. Reprinted by permission of the author and* Die Zeit. *Translated from the German by Gisela Savage and Birgitta Steene.*

In this particular scene, Ingmar Bergman's film *The Seventh Seal*,[1] which in a sinister and piercing way calls in question the existence of God, has its staggering climax. Not that there is any answer to be drawn from this. But there is certainty in death, certainty in the frailty of the body: this artfully arranged scene shows it, being at the same time so full of reality. It shows it in its concrete clarity which provokes no further interpretation. And it is precisely by putting the immediately tangible world, dying of the plague, on the screen, not only as symbol or allegory, but with terrifying reality that an ingenious director succeeds in giving the question of God's existence its hardness, its inevitability.

A knight, who returns to his plague-threatened country after a Crusade, plays a game of chess with Death. The time remaining for him to find an answer to his question is measured through the game. Foremost among the people he is still allowed to meet is a naive juggler whose simple mind is devoted to the supernatural. The miracle, the vision comes to the person who does not question. The questioning, however, (this ability to put forth seemingly logical arguments which prevents any possible knowledge of transcendence) is given to the squire Jöns, who in the face of death still talks cynically about "tremendous feelings" and "babbles of eternity" as comments to the outcry of the knight: "God, who exists somewhere, who must exist somewhere, have mercy on us!"

This controversy goes on throughout the entire film, disguised in various symbols. It is formulated once more in the end to accentuate the question of God in front of the dark figure of Death. The film itself does not give the answer. Death pulls the pawns with him in a sinister dance: away from dawn they move into night in a solemn dance, away into a secret land. This is how the amiably foolish juggler sees it in a vision that arouses the mockery of his wife.

What is stated here (though abridged: the meeting of the knight with the poor creature who is condemned as a witch is omitted) should be understood as an indication that this film is not an enlightening allegory but instead, with deep sincerity, poses the question of the meaning of our existence. This is a religious question

---

[1] [Although Bergman's film *Wild Strawberries* won a gold medal at the Berlin film festival in 1958, his breakthrough in Germany did not occur until after the showing of *Through a Glass Darkly* in 1962. Then a number of his films, among them *The Seventh Seal*, had their belated première in the Federal Republic.]

that encompasses the existence of God. It encompasses it, but it does not formulate it.

Bergman searches for the key. That is why he uses the form of a mystery play: it lends to the director, searching for truth and reality, the proper symbols to express his spiritual attitude. And the brilliance of this film lies in the fact that Bergman penetrates into a world of clear transcendental relationships, and does so from the standpoint of a modern, inquiring man; that he experiences this world, grasps it, and adapts it to our current consciousness of existence. He does this with such a passion that one should not hesitate to call this a religious film.

Bergman is concerned with death transforming man's existence and with man craving salvation. This creates consistently the style of the film. Throughout, there is tension between stylized structure and a tone of emotional exaggeration. The world of the knight and Death is austere, the agonizing madness of the people is expressive, while their fear as they succumb to the plague drives their faith to absurdity.

The film is ambivalent in an artful way. It mirrors reality—as far as we can imagine the Middle Ages—and at the same time gives its own strong spiritual definitions. The eye of the camera is always directed toward the symbolic, but at the same time contains details of a reality. The procession of flagellants is a real incident but also an eery spectacle that borders on the unbelievable.

However extraordinary it may seem it may be justified to draw a parallel with a sequence from Eisenstein's *The General Line*. In Eisenstein's film there is an ecstatic harvest procession of bearded priests, surrounded by smoldering incense and driven to the brink of grotesqueness. In this case the pathetic voice of the film submits itself to the ideology of atheism. The film becomes tendentious. The image is used by Eisenstein as well as by Bergman to express something which might be perceived beyond the concrete description of immediate reality.

Thus Bergman's film does not stand alone. To be sure, nothing connects it with the works of young contemporary directors, who quote reality from their immediate contact with it; who don't interpret life but merely strip it of all pretensions.

With many young directors today the answer is always secretly there. There is no use to try to penetrate the boundaries of our frail life. Such a philosophy of life brings about their cunning shirtsleeve realism. That, however, is the absolute antithesis of Bergman's film *The Seventh Seal*. Apocalypse and dance of death as grasped in their transcendental existence don't allow for an intellectually ironic distance. Instead we find in this film realism *and* distance of expression, both unveiling the essence of reality.

·◦⧸ ESSAYS ⧹◦·

A Program Note to
THE SEVENTH SEAL
by INGMAR BERGMAN

As a child I was sometimes allowed to accompany my father when he travelled about to preach in the small country churches in the vicinity of Stockholm. They were festive journeys, made by bicycle through a spring landscape. My father taught me the names of flowers, trees and birds. We spent the day in each other's company without being disturbed by the harassed world around us.

For a small boy the sermon itself of course is a matter purely for grown-ups. While Father preached away in the pulpit and the congregation prayed, sang or listened, I devoted my interest to the church's mysterious world of low arches, thick walls, the smell of eternity, the coloured sunlight quivering above the strangest vegetation of medieval paintings and carved figures on ceiling and walls. There was everything that one's imagination could desire: angels, saints, dragons, prophets, devils, humans. There were very frightening animals: serpents in paradise, Balaam's ass, Jonah's whale, the eagle of the Revelation. All this was surrounded by a heavenly, earthly and subterranean landscape of a strange yet familiar beauty. In a wood sat Death, playing chess with the Crusader. Clutching the branch of a tree was a naked man with staring eyes, while down below stood Death, sawing away to his heart's content. Across gentle hills Death led the final dance towards the dark lands.

But in the other arch the Holy Virgin was walking in a rose-garden, supporting the Child's faltering steps, and her hands were

Reprinted by permission of Ingmar Bergman and Svensk Film-industri. Translator not known.

those of a peasant woman. Her face was grave and birds' wings fluttered round her head.

The medieval painters had portrayed all this with great tenderness, skill and joy. It moved me in a spontaneous and enticing way, and that world became as real to me as the everyday world with Father, Mother and brothers and sisters.

On the other hand, I defended myself against the dimly sensed drama that was enacted in the crucifixion picture in the chancel. My mind was stunned by the extreme cruelty and the extreme suffering. Not until much later were faith and doubt become my constant companions.

It has been self-evident and profitable to give shape to the experiences of my childhood. I have been compelled to express the current dilemma.

My intention has been to paint in the same way as the medieval church painter, with the same objective interest, with the same tenderness and joy. My beings laugh, weep, howl, fear, speak, answer, play, suffer, ask, ask. Their terror is the plague, Judgment Day, the star whose name is Wormwood. Our fear is of another kind but our words are the same.

Our question remains.

Ingmar Bergman and the Black Death
by LARS-OLOF LÖTHWALL

> *And when he had opened the seventh
> seal, there was silence in heaven about
> the space of half an hour. And I saw the
> seven angels which stood before God;
> and to them were given seven trumpets.*
>
> (BOOK OF REVELATIONS, CHAPTER 8,
> VERSES 1–2).

The Black Death forms the gloomily suggestive background of Ingmar Bergman's latest film *The Seventh Seal*. "But that does not mean it is a somber Judgment Day film," one of his friends declares; "rather it is an unusually funny film for such a serious subject. . . ."

It would probably be going too far to liken Bergman to Shakespeare but the two bear a certain resemblance. Bergman too is the amazingly confident magician, who can toss around any subject matter simply and perfectly. In one film he blows happy soap bubbles around love and eroticism, in another he is the doomsday prophet, and in this film he has turned his ability to a ballad about the Middle Ages.

This sounds strange to us who, like fussy schoolmistresses, have learnt to look upon the Middle Ages as a dark and superstitious age, as a painful but necessary scene in the drama of world history.

But Ingmar has a different opinion! (He has almost always different opinions!).

—Laughter was the great liberator of the Middle Ages. It was the safety valve against the pressure from above and below—

"Ingmar Bergman och Digerdöden" by Lars-Olof Löthwall. From Stockholms-Tidningen, *July 5, 1956. Reprinted by permission of the author. Translated from the Swedish by Birgitta Steene.*

fear of God and fear of the Devil. Both parties painted Old Nick on the wall—in different shapes. People dared not protest—only laugh: sometimes. The faint smile does not belong to that time but the boisterous guffaw.

The literary background of *The Seventh Seal* is Bergman's own play *Wood Painting*. But the film is not photographed theater; Ingmar Bergman is too much of a cinematic genius for that. *The Seventh Seal* is an entirely new product, with Bergman bearing in mind, all the time, the expressive means of celluloid.

—I have fused *Wood Painting* with other ideas, images, and thoughts. For five months I rewrote the script five times, hidden in a small room in the gatekeeper's cabin in the film city.

—*The Seventh Seal* is an entirely new attempt on my part, an unusual film in a new genre which I am convinced is cinematic. *The Seal* will not be like anything anyone else has ever done. This does not mean that I chase originality for its own sake, but that I am trying to find new cinematic means of expression.

—The art of the film must not stand still; no art must stagnate. I want to paint in a simple and quite unpretentious manner in black and white. I have no desire to try color film, for it is not yet genuine. So far it is no more than sickly sweet candy to the eye.

The Seventh Seal has no frame story. It takes place one day in July of 1350, the day when the knight plays chess with Death, with life as his stake, and when a troupe of actors travels through the district. In their footpath the plague, the Black Death, follows, silent but terrible.

A cue:

—They talk of the Judgment Day. And all these omens are certainly terrible. Down in the village a woman gave birth to a calf's head, and worms and chopped-off hands began pouring out of an old woman.

And in the church porch a wood painting tells about Man, Death, and the Devil. . . .

The shooting of *The Seventh Seal* has started just recently in Svensk Filmindustri's film city at Råsunda, where architect P. A. Lundgren has created a medieval inn—the Embarrassment Inn.

A pig is hanging on the spit above the fire, now with a sickening smell after a couple of days of takes. The floor is of trampled dirt and the poor people are sitting along the walls. They are played by extras whom Ingmar and his assistant Lennart Olsson have found in old-age homes; one after another to do his silent part. There are a couple of old men crouching in a corner, a cripple is crawling on the floor together with a pig, and a blind man sits quietly on a bench. In another corner some children are staring with big eyes at what is happening.

No health authority has been ravaging here with its legal paragraphs—the milieu is stinking and dirty, but genuine. What a wonderful breeding ground for a plague!

In this repugnant smell the Evil people mix with the Good and the Indifferent. The little subdued juggler Jof (Nils Poppe) is dancing under threats and taunts on a table until he can no longer endure it.

He falls down, perspiration spurts forth, and he pants, almost driven to death:

—I cannot be a bear any more, I cannot, I cannot . . .

His torturer (Bertil Anderberg) is impossible to stop, he grabs a torch and pushes it towards Jof's eyes. The smith (Åke Fridell) takes a beer mug and pours it over Jof. Then . . .

Then enters the squire Jöns (Gunnar Björnstrand), horrible to observe in his crewcut and with a terrible scar on his head. He retaliates—with a knife he disfigures the face of Jof's torturer. . . .

Jof runs away. . . .

For Ingmar the only thing that exists now is *The Seventh Seal*. He lives only in that film and for it. Everything else is dismissed to a sphere of unreality. No new film, no stage play, nothing but this film is worth talking about.

Yet I ask him what his plans are.

The answer comes like a whiplash:

FILM! But who knows how much longer we can afford to make movies in Sweden? Our absolutely insane taxation and the ever-increasing production costs make every shooting a daring venture. Five or six years ago this film would have cost 250,000 Sw. crowns [$50,000]. Today we estimate the expenses at 500,000 [$100,000].

This is the Black Death of the cinema.

THE SEVENTH SEAL
by BOSLEY CROWTHER

While the ferment of cinema creation was bubbling in many countries after the Second World War, there was in Sweden a young man whose destiny was to restore the fame of Swedish motion pictures to the eminence they had enjoyed during the "golden age" of Mauritz Stiller and Victor Sjöström, between 1918 and 1925.

This young man was Ingmar Bergman, a name that sounded so much like that of the famous Swedish actress, Ingrid Bergman, that for several years, even after his own fame was established, he was often referred to flippantly as "Sweden's other Bergman." That isn't done any more.

Bergman, whose childhood and boyhood were spent under the stern eye of a Lutheran-minister father, broke into motion pictures in 1944 as a scriptwriter. His first script, for a picture called *Hets* (*Torment*), told a suspiciously intimate tale of a schoolboy tormented by a sadistic teacher to the point where his life was almost ruined. The next year, he began directing and went through a period of several years in which he wrote and directed a variety of pictures in a variety of styles.

The titles—*Crisis, Prison, Illicit Interlude, The Naked Night*—signpost a spate of heavy dramas, solemn and tormented things in which the maturing Bergman worked out his agonies and hates. Then suddenly he did an about face and followed with three comedies. The third one, a sparkling charmer, sophisticated and erotic, called *Smiles of a Summer Night,* won a special commendation at the Cannes Film Festival in 1956. Bergman, up till then a nobody—outside his own country, at least—was now recognized as

From The Great Films: Fifty Golden Years of Motion Pictures *by Bosley Crowther (New York: G. P. Putnam's Sons, 1967), pp. 218–22. Copyright © 1967 by Bosley Crowther. Reprinted by permission of the author and the publisher.*

a writer-director who gave promise of following in the old Ernst Lubitsch vein.

But his very next picture confounded all expectation of such a thing and served notice that here was a cinema creator of extraordinary range and magnitude. For that next picture was his philosophical and poetic allegory, *The Seventh Seal*, which was immediately hailed as a triumph and is now established as a screen masterpiece.

The strong intellectual passion of it took viewers by surprise, mainly because such powerful brooding as it contains was so unusual in latter-day films. In a sense, it is in the great tradition of Strindberg and Selma Lagerlöf, deep probers of man's inner nature, and it follows in the philosophical line of the films that were made by Stiller and Sjöström in the early days. Indeed, it is evident that Bergman has been very strongly moved by the strange contemplative nature of the great Swedish silent films. He has acknowledged himself in the tradition, and has said that *The Seventh Seal* was inspired by the film that Sjöström made from Lagerlöf's *The Phantom Chariot* in 1920. That, too, was a fantasy-allegory in which man was confronted by Death and placed the strength of his virtue in conflict with the forces of doom.

The Seventh Seal is essentially the story of a lonely man's search for God—or, perhaps it might better be said, the story of a man's search for meaning in life. Its hero is seeking the Answer. "I want knowledge, not belief," he cries, "not faith, not suppositions, but knowledge!" This ageless cry of anguish is the theme of only a few great films. And the extraordinary thing about this one is the forcefulness with which it conveys the magnitude of its abstract ideas with visual images, the manner in which it makes you fathom the loneliness of man, the mystery of God, the fearful shadow that lies between life and death, the hideousness of superstition, and the piteousness of blind faith.

The specified time of its action is the fourteenth century and the locale is Sweden or Denmark, a primitive, rude, and forested land that is suffering a terrible epidemic of bubonic plague. It begins with a knight, returning from the Crusades, met on the rocky, wind-lashed coast by a black-robed, chalk-faced figure who announces himself to be Death. Death is waiting to take him, as he is taking so many in the land, but the knight bids for time to do a good deed and make one final attempt to fathom life. He challenges Death to a chess game on condition that he may live as long as he avoids a checkmate. If he wins, he will be released.

And so, while the game is in progress (which it is, as shown in cut-back scenes throughout the film), the knight and his squire, a wholesome skeptic, go riding through the land observing the behavior of the people under the lurking menace of doom. Some are giving themselves to cruel self-torture under the brutish soldiers who whip the people into line. Others, a group of seeming wardens, are preparing to burn a girl as a "witch," on the clearly preposterous charge that she has trafficked with the Devil.

Still others, scornful of religion, are wallowing in pleasure like pigs, feasting and fornicating, or ribaldly amusing themselves by watching an entertainment put on by a tiny strolling troupe. But in this band of players, the knight and his faithful squire, both of them weary and cynical of meaningless mouthings about God, find three innocent persons—a juggler, his wife, and their infant child—who are as simple, fresh, and wholesome as the morning dew. Except that the juggler sees visions, bright illusions, from time to time (to his pretty wife's tolerant amusement), the happy couple are as normal as their child. They are the concentration of simplicity, love, and purity.

And so it is this little family that the knight, still unsatisfied in his quest for understanding, arranges to have elude the destruction of Death at the climax, when he and a piteous band of wanderers he has picked up must surrender themselves to Death at the end of the game.

Of course, one may see this picture as nothing more than a Gothic fantasy, a fearful descriptive visualization of morbid and medieval horrors. And there is enough horror and ugliness in it to make the blood run cold. Bergman is a passionate zealot for frank, realistic imagery, and his pictorial presentations of a people whose bodies and minds are diseased by corruption and ignorance are more eloquent than any words.

For instance, his scene of a procession of religious masochists—a gaggle of hollow, howling creatures, some dismally hooded and cowled, some staggering under the weight of mammoth crosses, some lashing themselves with thongs; crippled, diseased, and maniacal—that comes straggling over a hill, marshaled by priests and soldiers, pacing to a grim, liturgical chant, is a scene right out of the Dark Ages. Indeed, Bergman took his cue for its design from old paintings on Swedish church walls.

Or his scene of the preparation to burn the girl at the stake is a blood-chilling documentation of human savagery. There's the child, paralyzed with terror, the fright of hell in her staring eyes, resigned long since to her ordeal, while callow men go about the task of piling wood on a platform and lighting the unrelenting fire. The scene can only be compared to the fine one of a witch-burning in Carl Th. Dreyer's impressive Danish film, *Day of Wrath* (1948).

Yes, there is plenty of horror in this picture—and intentionally, be it said, because Bergman believes in involving the emotions of his viewers with shocks. He has stated without hesitation that he cannot abide that his films be exposed to "the merely indifferent presence of a popcorn-chewing audience."

But it should be obvious that there is much more in it than sheer Gothic fantasy. It should be obvious that the knight is intended as a symbol of modern man, a modern intellectual, such as Bergman himself. He is weary of war, disillusioned about serving an unknown God that permits the injustices, cruelties, and sufferings that occur in the world, and shocked by man's fear and trembling in the face of prophesied doom—in this case the plague, which plainly symbolizes the nuclear bomb.

Likewise, it should be obvious that the characters met by the knight and his squire in their patient traveling toward the knight's long-unvisited home are symbols of various types of humans. There's the crude actor in the strolling troupe who shirks his responsibility to go leching after the blacksmith's wife. There's the latter, a lusty, selfish woman, full of deceit and fickleness; and there's her husband, a harmless dullard who contributes nothing but muscle to the world.

More significant, there is a perfidious exseminarian who robs, cheats, and bullies the pure and helpless. And there is a fiery-eyed minister who shouts about doom and damnation and fills his listeners with fear of God, not love. These rascals symbolize the treachery of religious teachers, just as the awesome parade of masochists is symbolic of enslavement to ritualized beliefs. At one point, the knight complains darkly, "We make an idol of our fear and call it God."

To be sure, there are other symbols, others aspects, that are not too clear, and this has been one of the reasons for some criticism of

the film. What precisely is the idea behind the character of Death?
Is it but the end of existence of each individual? If it is—if that's
all one can fathom from this complicated film—then it is indeed
shallow and romantic and Bergman might be called immature.

But I see Death as much more than a warder who simply rings
down the curtain on life. He, or it, is a sort of cosmic conscience
that every man must confront. Death is the constant observer who
challenges every one of us, watching our every action, demanding
our measuring up, and ready to lead us to oblivion when we have
played our games and lost. Thus Death takes each of the characters
who symbolizes some weakness or error, some one of the human
deficiencies that are dispensable in the world. But Death does not
get the juggler, his wife, and their infant child because these people
possess the virtues of purity and generosity that must not die.

Actually, Death as an assassin is not the antagonist. The antagonist is the moral and spiritual condition of man. It is this, the state
of evil that man has allowed to occur, that confronts the knight
throughout his wanderings and causes him to question God. Death
is the visual presentation of the device by which man is erased—
that is to say, the conscience—that takes all but the pure in the end.

Many techniques and tendencies of Bergman are richly revealed
in this film—his use of natural beauty, for instance. His camera is
quick to catch the aesthetic essence of nature, whether it be in the
cold and rocky coast, swept by strong winds from off the ocean and
pounded by the sea, or in the immediately juxtaposed radiance of
an early morn. His sensitive use of nature distills a strongly characteristic poetry. And especially so because he puts it in sharp contrast
to other elements that communicate the aberrations and artificiali-
ties of man in the social state. For instance, there is a simple, exquisite moment in *The Seventh Seal*: Death has sawed down the
tree into which the deceitful actor, Skat, has tried to flee, showing
in one awesome image the fate of this wickedness. Then, onto the
tree stump, in close-up, leaps a tiny squirrel with bright, beady eyes,
all charm and innocence. This is nature compensating for ruin.

Now a word for the acting. Bergman has regularly drawn from a
small group of excellent Swedish actors for the casts of his films.
Their frequent collaborations with him and his knowledge of their
individual skills have made for an ideal condition of creative give
and take.

Here he has Max von Sydow as the knight, a tall, thin man,

exuding the strength, the stoicism and the inner spiritual fervor of the Swedes; and Gunnar Björnstrand, who has been a performer in more Bergman films than anyone else, has the prize role of the incisive, sardonic, implacable squire. Nils Poppe is charming as the bright-eyed and bouncy little juggler who goes free, and Bibi Andersson is delicious as his wholesome, adoring wife.

After this classic picture, Bergman went on to make a succession of brilliant screen dramas—the nostalgic *Wild Strawberries,* for which he had aged Victor Sjöström play the leading role; *Brink of Life*; *The Magician*; the rightly moralistic *The Virgin Spring*. And then he embarked upon a morbid and deeply contemplative trilogy, in which he returned to the theme of the anguish of the individual who feels lost or neglected in a search for God. Bergman persists in being a believer, although publicly tortured by doubt, and he maintains that every drama should in some way attempt to clarify the relation of man to God. "I will never give up the discussion," he has solemnly proclaimed.

Yet I doubt that he will ever make a picture that will surpass *The Seventh Seal* as a cosmic contemplation of the eternal man-God theme. And I am sure that he will never catch an image that will move me, at least, any more than the scene at the end, wherein Death leads a saraband of the departed souls of the drama across a hilltop against a clouded sky.

THE SEVENTH SEAL

by ANDREW SARRIS

"And when he had opened the seventh seal, there was silence in heaven about the space of half an hour."

"REVELATION"

"A free mind, like a creative imagination, rejoices at the harmonies it can find or make between man and nature; and where it finds none, it solves the conflict so far as it may and then notes and endures it with a shudder."

GEORGE SANTAYANA,
"ART AND HAPPINESS"

Although Ingmar Bergman's *The Seventh Seal* is set in medieval Sweden, nothing could be more modern than its author's conception of death as the crucial reality of man's existence. Appearing at a time when the anguished self-consciousness of Kierkegaard and Nietzsche has come back into favor as a statement of the human condition, *The Seventh Seal* is perhaps the first genuinely existential film. The plight of the individual in an indifferent universe would have seemed a fatuous subject for an artist a generation ago when human objectives barely extended to the next bread line, and when, it now seems ages ago, Edmund Wilson could reasonably denounce Thornton Wilder's metaphysical concerns in *The Bridge of San Luis Rey* as socially irresponsible. Liberal reform, Marxist determinism, and the Social Gospel of Christianity were variously hailed as the formulas of a blissful world, but something went wrong with these collective panaceas partly because thinking men discovered that endless problem-solving reduced life to its one insoluble problem, death,

"The Seventh Seal" *by Andrew Sarris. From* Film Culture *19 (1959):51–61. Reprinted by permission of the author and* Film Culture.

and partly because population explosions, the hydrogen bomb, and the Cold War scuttled the idea of Progress as a cause for rejoicing. Quite obviously, the time has come to talk of other things beside the glories of social reconstruction.

Ingmar Bergman, the son of a clergyman, is aware of the decline of religious faith in the modern world, but unlike Dreyer, he refuses to reconstruct mystic consolations from the dead past. If modern man must live without the faith which makes death meaningful, he can at least endure life with the aid of certain necessary illusions. This is what Bergman seems to be saying in *The Seventh Seal,* a remarkably intricate film with many layers of meaning.

The Biblical context of the Seventh Seal is never fully retold on the screen, but enough excerpts are provided to keynote the theme of the Last Judgment. A hawk [see note p. 9] suspended in flight opens the film with a striking image of foreboding against a rising chorale of exultant faith. After ten years on a Crusade to the Holy Land, a knight and his squire return disillusioned to Sweden. Riding north to the knight's castle further and further away from Christianity's birthplace where God has died in their hearts, the knight and the squire are cast allegorically into the void of modern disbelief.

They first appear on a lonely beach, the knight seated by his chessboard, the squire flung awkwardly in a lackey's sleep. The two horses prance against the rushing waves as sun, sky, and sea converge on the distant horizon. In the midst of a dazzling progression of sun-setting dissolves, the black-hooded figure of Death confronts the blond knight. Bergman's editing is ambiguous here for one cannot be sure that Death has actually materialized out of space. Nor is there any camera trickery involved in Death's subsequent manifestations. Death is presumably too real for magic lantern effects.

The knight challenges Death to a game of chess, the knight's life to be staked on the outcome. As the game begins with Death taking the black pieces, Bergman composes the first of his many tableaux inspired by medieval church murals. Death and the knight resume their match at fixed dramatic intervals later in the film. Bergman's fable is shaped by this chess game, not so much in the symbolism of the moves, most notably Death takes knight, but in the expanding meanings and ambiguities of the two players. While seeking God in the world of men, the knight relentlessly pursues the enigma of his antagonist.

As the knight and the squire continue their homeward journey, towering overhead shots of the two riders alternate with pulsating images of the sun. This cosmic technique would be pretentious for a lesser theme, but here in the beginning, Bergman is suggesting the dimensions of the universe in which his drama will unfold. Once the philosophical size of the film is established, Bergman's camera probes more intimately into his characters.

The fact that the squire does not share the knight's first encounter with Death is consistent with Bergman's conception of the knight's solitude in his quest for God. Since the squire is a confirmed atheist, the knight cannot seek consolation in that quarter. Indeed, the squire's bawdy songs and low comedy grimaces stamp him as the knight's Sancho Panza until a startling incident transforms him into a coprotagonist. Dismounting to ask a hooded stranger the way to the next town, the squire lifts the hood and beholds the death skull of a plague victim. The squire's reaction is that of a forceful intelligence, and he displays an unexpected flair for irony when he tells the unsuspecting knight that the stranger said nothing but was quite eloquent. Bergman achieves his shock effect here with the aid of a dog frisking about its dead master before the squire lifts the man's hood. This is more than a trick, however, and Bergman later develops the flickering idea involved here.

Bergman adds to his chess pieces as the knight and the squire ride past a carnival wagon in which an actor, a juggler, the juggler's wife, and their infant son are asleep. Emerging from the wagon into a sunlit world less intensely illuminated than the world of the knight and the squire, the juggler is awed by a vision of the Virgin Mary walking the Christ Child. He calls his wife to describe this latest miracle of his imaginative existence, and as always, she is kind but skeptical. (Bergman has a priceless talent for establishing states of being in quick scenes.) The juggler and his wife are suggestively named Jof and Mia at slight variance from an explicit identification with Christ's parents. They are never quite that, but when Joseph observes wistfully that his son, Michael, will perform the one impossible juggling trick, the screen vibrates with Bergman's first intimations of immortality.

Bergman returns to his central theme as the actor steps out of the wagon to announce that he will play Death in the religious pageant at Elsinore. Donning a death mask, he asks (vanity of vanities!) if the women will still admire him in that disguise. As the pompous director of the troupe, he orders Joseph to portray the Soul of Man, a part Joseph dislikes for theatrical reasons. When the actor returns to the wagon, hanging the death skull on a pole outside, the camera lingers on this symbol long enough for the sound track to record the pleasant laughter of Jof and Mia before cutting back to the couple whose merriment operates both as a conscious reaction to the departing actor and as the director's expression of their irreverent attitude towards death. In all this symbolic by-play, Jof and Mia convey a wondrous innocence, and the scene ends on a note of emotional recollection as Mia's avowal of her love for her husband is underscored by the same musical motif which accompanied Jof's vision of the Madonna.

Bergman shifts from the sunlit innocence of the carnival wagon to the ominous atmosphere of a medieval church. While the knight pursues his quest for God at the altar of Christ, the squire exchanges blasphemies with a morbidly cynical church painter whose fearsome murals of the Dance of Death, the Black Plague, and religious flagellations are the visual inspiration of *The Seventh Seal*. This circular recognition of a predecessor typifies Bergman's concern with the role of art in transcending the existential limits of human life.

Unable to find solace at the altar, the knight advances towards a hooded figure in the confessional chamber. The knight's unrecognized confessor is Death, and in an electrifying passage of self-revelation, the knight confesses all the agony of a mortal man seeking God while unwilling to embrace a religion of fear. Death, the confessor, offers no consolation, no guarantees, no answers, and in his tactical role, lures the knight into revealing his chess strategy.

The knight's outrage when he discovers the deception may well be shared by the audience. Why should Death cheat on certainties? It is possible that Bergman is intensifying the horror of life by suggesting ultimate nothingness with intermediate stages of accident and caprice. Since Death's timing follows no logical pattern, he might as well indulge in masquerades and linger over interesting chess games. Bergman suggests also that Death is everywhere—the church, the confessional chamber, perhaps even on the Cross.

The knight achieves heroic stature in his reaction to Death's hoax. Extending his hands before him to feel the blood pulsing in his veins, noting the sun still at its zenith, the suddenly exultant knight proclaims to his hitherto uncertain self the one certainty of an appointment to play chess with Death. Almost any other director would have sustained this great cinematic moment with either an immense close-up or a receding tracking shot to the ceiling of the church looking down upon mortal man in his fullest affirmation. Instead, Bergman truncates his effect with a quick cut to the squire entertaining the church painter with a Rabelaisian account of the Crusade. This abrupt transition from sublimity to ridicule is characteristic of Bergman's balanced treatment of the high-low dualism of human life.

From this point on, the fear-ridden world impinges upon the knight and the squire. The Black Plague is now seen sweeping across Sweden on a trail of hysteria, witch-burnings, and religious flagellations. The knight asks a young woman condemned for witchcraft to lead him to the Devil, who might confirm the existence of God. The knight is answered only by a piteous wail which evokes the callous inhumanity of the period. The squire rescues a silent girl from a renegade priest who has degenerated into a robber of the dead. Ironically, this same priest, the closest human equivalent of evil in *The Seventh Seal,* once shamed the knight into embarking on the Crusade.

The various threads of the plot are woven together into the fabric of a town which represents for Bergman many of the evils of society. Art reappears in a musical pantomime of cuckoldry presented by Jof, Mia, and the preening actor. The medieval approximation which Bergman attempts in this performance is carried over into the actor's flamboyant affair with a flirtatious blacksmith's wife. With dainty steps and cock-robin flourishes, the seduction in the nearby forest derives its tempo from a bawdy nonsense song rendered in the town by Jof and Mia, their faces gaily painted, their manner joyously abandoned. Their performance is meaningfully interrupted by the wailing of flagellants bearing Christ on the Cross. Bergman cuts with brilliant deliberation back and forth between the painful detail of the incense-shrouded procession and tracking shots of the soldiers and townspeople kneeling reverently in turn as the Cross goes past. The same soldiers who threw fruit at the actors (art) now kneel to their Saviour (fear).

The brutalization of a fear-crazed society reaches its climax in an inn where the patrons suspend their discourses on the End of the World to laugh sadistically at Jof's grotesque dance on a table while the renegade priest brandishes a torch at the juggler's feet. (The ordeal of a performer deprived of his mask and the sanctuary

of his stage is more fully explored in Bergman's *The Naked Night*.)
Joseph [Jof] escapes only because of the intervention of the squire,
who slashes the priest's face. In a film drenched with death, this is
the only instance in which blood is drawn.

Withdrawing from the discord of the town, the knight is moved
by the innocent contentment of Jof and Mia to offer them his protection and the sanctuary of his castle. The knight, the squire, and
the silent girl share with the juggler's family an interlude of resignation. The knight consecrates this moment in his memory with sacramental bowls of milk and wild strawberries, Bergman's personal
symbols of the bread and wine of human redemption. The final
movement of *The Seventh Seal* is then performed in a forest of unearthly calm and tempest, and a castle of last judgement.

The knight's caravan takes on the spiritual contours of an Ark in
a drowning world. Having assumed responsibility for Jof's family,
the knight is now engaged in a selfless cause. The squire's instinctive
humanism has gained him the loyalty of the silent girl he has rescued
and the friendship of the cuckolded blacksmith he has pitied. Yet,
the growing intimacy of the characters is itself an ominous portent
of Death.

The rising tension is checked momentarily by an encounter with
the errant blacksmith's wife and the actor. Here Bergman provides
the last bawdy counterpoint to his major theme as the blacksmith
is reconciled to his wife while the actor feigns suicide with a stage
dagger. This apparently gratuitous scene is a fitting prelude to
Death's manifestation in the forest. When the actor climbs a tree to
be safe from the wood animals during the night only to see Death
saw down this medieval tree of life, the dark comedy of the incident
confirms Bergman's sense of structure. The buffoonery of actor-
blacksmith-wife is the film's last semblance of life unconcerned with
death, and it is required for Bergman's graded shocks. However, one
is suspended between horror and humor as the tree comes down
with the actor screaming soundlessly and a squirrel hopping on to
the stump chirping loudly. This image of animal life in the presence
of human death expands the notion of individual mortality which
Bergman touched upon in his earlier conjunction of the dog and
the plague victim.

The caravan next encounters the witch, who is to be burned in
the forest. Still searching for God, the knight asks her once more
for the whereabouts of the Devil. The girl raves that the Devil is in

1. Ingmar Bergman, about 1957. Photo courtesy Janus Films, Inc.

2. Max von Sydow as the Knight, Antonius Block.

3. Death greeting the Knight on the shore.

4. Death and the Knight at the chess board.

5. Bibi Andersson as Mia and Nils Poppe as her husband, Jof.

6. The witch in the stocks outside the church.

7. Jof, Mia, and Skat performing a pantomime.

8. The train of flagellants.

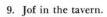
9. Jof in the tavern.

10. Feasting on strawberries and milk on the hillside.

11. The Knight and his companions facing Death at the end.

12. Death leading "the solemn dance toward the dark lands. . . ."

her eyes, but the knight perceives only the reflection of her terror. When he asks an attending monk why the girl's hands have been broken, the monk who turns his face is Death, now cynically inquiring when the knight will stop asking questions. In this stunning moment of recognition, the knight's destiny is revealed. He must continue his quest despite its futility.

Although the knight has given the witch a drug to ease her pain, her last moments on the stake are filled with wild despair as she realizes that the Devil is not going to claim her from the emptiness which lies beyond the flames. The squire confronts the knight for the first time with evidence (?) of the void, but the knight refuses to abandon hope. One would lose all sympathy for Bergman's characters if they treated the witch's ordeal as merely a test of God's existence. Fortunately, Bergman never loses his human perspective on death even when the renegade priest is stricken by the Plague. The silent girl he once menaced rushes towards him until the squire restrains her, virtually pleading that any help would be futile. Dying never becomes a casual process for Bergman. The actor, the witch, the renegade priest all achieve a form of moral purgation in the inescapable self-pity they arouse in their audiences, both real and fictitious.

When Death confronts the knight for the final moves on the chessboard, the once stark tonal contrasts between the two antagonists have merged into relativistic grayness. Gone is the sun and the sea and the sky. Death has enveloped the forest and no longer makes striking entrances with his black cloak. Jof "sees" Death at the chessboard and takes flight with Mia and Michael. Fearing Death's intervention, the knight knocks over the pieces to allow Jof and his family to escape. Inscrutable to the end, Death does not indicate whether he has been taken in by this diversion, or whether he is tolerant or indifferent, or whether, after all, he *is* actually controlled by a Higher Power. Once Death has achieved checkmate and has claimed the knight and his friends at the next meeting, he still denies he possesses any secrets of the afterlife, and in a dissolving close-up, his face is slowly and memorably transformed into a hollow mask.

While Jof and Mia are fleeing Death's storm in the forest, the knight leads his remaining companions into his castle where the knight's wife waits alone, a medieval Penelope who seems as weary of life as does her tortured husband. Here Bergman resists the beguiling temptation to sentimentalize the knight's attitude towards death. Having performed a noble service for Jof and Mia and having retained his wife's love for the ten years sacrificed in a futile search for God, the knight might be allowed to meet Death with the lofty grandeur with which most doomed film heroes crash into oblivion. Instead, when Death appears at the long banquet table to claim the knight and his guests, the knight prays hopelessly and, at last, unconditionally, to a God who must exist if life is not to end in senseless terror. The squire remains true to his own colors as he scoffs at the knight's quest for God. Accepting Death under protest, the squire acclaims his life without God, but significantly the last words are spoken by the silent girl: "It is finished."

This elliptical declaration of awareness, perhaps miraculously extracted from the text of Revelation, is less meaningful than the glowing expression in her eyes as she awaits the end of her earthly servitude. The silent girl, more than any of the other characters, has been defeated by life, and in her defeat, has embraced the prospect of death. When we first see her, she is about to be raped and murdered. She passively accepts her role as the squire's housekeeper, and is always seen either bearing some burden or accepting the squire's protection. One almost suspects Bergman of a class statement in his conception of this memorable, yet elusive, character.

Yet, all of Death's victims in the forest and the castle have failed in some way. The actor is impaled on his vanity; the witch deluded into a pointless martyrdom by the ignorance of society; the renegade priest stripped of the last vestiges of self-induced consolation; the knight tortured by endless doubt; the squire limited to the easy wisdom and cynicism of the world; the blacksmith and his wife enmeshed in trivialities; the knight's wife deprived of the passion which might once have resisted Death. Strangely, there is little sense of regret. None of Death's victims ever suggest that they would have lived their lives differently if they had another chance. The knight is not even sorry that he embarked on the Crusade. One hesitates to suggest predestination in such an agnostic context, but it is difficult to recall significant opportunities for moral choice in any of Bergman's films released thus far in America.

When Jof and Mia emerge once more into the sunlight, the Black Cloud of Death is safely past. (Some critics have translated this cloud into the H-bomb, but the analogy is both labored and unnecessary. More substantial social parallels can be derived from the scenes of fear and doubt; the squire's description of his outlook as "modern" is deliciously ironic.) Against the distant sky, Jof sees the Dance of Death, Bergman's majestic summation of medieval imagery. As Death leads his six victims, hand to hand, in the fierce merriment of their last revels, *The Seventh Seal* soars to the heights of imaginative cinema.

It is not until Jof describes the Dance of Death that we realize that his vision is inspired by a creative imagination rather than a Divine Revelation. The people he identifies in the Dance of Death —Death, the knight, the squire, the actor, the blacksmith and his wife, and the renegade priest—are not entirely the same people Death confronts in the castle. Jof has never seen the knight's wife, and her absence from his vision is quite logical. The omission of the silent girl is more puzzling. At least two interesting theories suggest themselves. The silent girl's final expression of acceptance slowly dissolves into the watchful expression of Mia. The two women look very much alike, and whatever this means—Jof developing a mental block in imagining death for someone resembling Mia, Jof unconsciously admiring the silent girl, Jof even absent-mindedly overlooking the existence of this girl—a clear link has been established between these two archetypes of woman.

The second theory is almost frighteningly intellectual. Since Jof calls off the names of the Dancers, it is possible that the unnamed silent girl cannot operate in Jof's artistic imagination. Except for the witch, all the other recurring characters are assigned proper names, but the silent girl, like the witch, remains an abstract being beyond Jof's ability to recall in his creations. This theory raises the question of Bergman's immersion in the technical philosophies of logical and linguistic analysis, a question which can be answered ultimately only by Bergman himself. Yet, it is quite clear from his interviews and his past films that he has been influenced by the irrational ideas of illusion and existence expressed in the works of Camus, Sartre, Anouilh, Strindberg, and Pirandello.

If Jof and Mia represent the continuity of man, they do so because of certain transcendent illusions—love, art, contentment, and the future of their child. These futile distractions from imminent death make life endurable if not justifiable. Yet, the knight and the squire are also aspects of man, the knight as the questing mystic, the squire as the earthbound philosopher. It is possible to identify Bergman in some measure with all three characters since *The*

Seventh Seal is a unique amalgam of beauty, mysticism, and rational logic. What is most remarkable about Bergman's achievement is that he projects the most pessimistic view of human existence with an extraordinary vitality. Conceding that life is hell and death is nothingness, he still imparts to the screen a sense of joy in the very futility of man's illusions.

For all its intellectual complexity, *The Seventh Seal* is remarkably entertaining. In the high level of acting we have come to expect in Bergman films, Gunnar Björnstrand as the squire, and Bengt Ekerot as Death, provide truly remarkable performances. Björnstrand, previously seen here in *The Naked Night* and *Smiles of a Summer Night*, displays classic range in the subtlety and force of his widely dissimilar characterizations. Bengt Ekerot's playing of Death is so uncanny that it is difficult to imagine this unfamiliar actor in any other role. Max von Sydow has the most difficult part as the mystical knight who must communicate from the depths of his soul, but in his dramatic scenes, he fully captures the tortured nobility of his character. Nils Poppe, Sweden's leading comedian, is very moving as Jof through the counterpoint of his comic personality and his cosmic problems. Bibi Andersson as Mia heads a gallery of unaffectedly beautiful women which includes anonymous faces in Bergman's crowd scenes.

Bergman's camera technique is fully equal to his theme. Except for a glaring process shot in the opening scene, his medieval images are clear and solid in the best tradition of realistic cinematography. Bergman is at his best in intimate scenes where his unobtrusively moving camera builds up tensions before his editing exploits them. One is always aware of the meaningful texture of faces as they react to the uncertainties they confront. Bergman indulges in the sun dissolves endemic to Swedish cinema, and the reverse cloak opening of a frame which Hitchcock invented, but which Bergman gives a special flourish in many of his films. In this instance, Death's black cloak must have been irresistible.

Bergman's overall editing maintains a steady flow of images to create visual progressions for each successive plot development. The plastic symbol of the death skull reappears in each shot at a different expressive angle, and Death himself never repeats the choreography of his comings and goings. Bergman's economy of expression actually makes it difficult to absorb all the meanings in each scene. Instead of fully developing his ideas in long, obligatory confrontations of characters, Bergman distributes fragments of what he is saying into every incident. Yet, a great deal that is implied is left unsaid, and it is possible that *The Seventh Seal* will be a source of controversy for years to come, and that like all classics of the mind, its interpretations will vary with the minds and times of its critics.

THE SEVENTH SEAL:
An Existential Vision
by BIRGITTA STEENE

The Seventh Seal begins with the sound track transmitting the resonant voices of a church choir. Then the singing suddenly stops and there is absolute silence. The camera moves in upon the knight who is waking up, and glides over the face of Jöns, who lies asleep with gaping mouth. The time is early morning; the light is gray and nature seems to lie in a coma.

After a prayer, the knight stares into the morning sun, which wallows up from the misty sea "like some bloated dying fish" to quote from Bergman's literary script. High above the infinite ocean a sea-eagle is floating on its wings. This scene is not merely a piece of cinematic exposition; it is a thematic prelude: in the image of the gliding bird seen against a sky which is "a dome of lead," Bergman telescopes the knight's hopeless search for God, who remains distant and silent.

A voice, which now begins to read a brief passage from the Revelation of St. John the Divine, speaks directly to the knight, who fails to understand its message. But the passage also puts the title of the film into context. God's Book of Secrets is to be imagined as a scroll of parchment with seven seals. Not until the seventh seal is broken will man know the secret of life: "And when he had opened the seventh seal, there was a silence in heaven about the space of half an hour." Bergman's film can be regarded as a visualization of that half hour during which man may prepare himself for the ultimate truth.

From Ingmar Bergman *by Birgitta Steene (New York: Twayne Publishers, Inc., 1968), pp. 61–69. Copyright © 1968 by Twayne Publishers, Inc. Reprinted by permission of the publisher.*

As the voice reads, the camera shifts its angle; high aerial shots from the cliffs above the beach depict an absolutely desolate country. Thus, we are prepared for the actual figure of Death, which appears next on the screen. With his immobile, white face and wide, black coat, the actor's personification of Death suggests a Grand Guignol figure. The knight, however, is never surprised by his meeting with Death and, except once, Bergman never lets Death be visible to the audience while being invisible to Antonius Block.

Although the knight's quest is medieval, his skeptic and anxious temper is modern. To help justify such an anachronism Bergman claims that the medieval world depicted in *The Seventh Seal* is basically a historical metaphor for our own world threatened by atomic destruction: "In my film the Crusader returns from the Crusades as the soldier returns from the war today. In the Middle Ages, men lived in terror of the plague. Today they live in fear of the atomic bomb. *The Seventh Seal* is an allegory with a theme that is quite simple: man, his eternal search for God, with death as his only certainty."

Bergman's use of the term "allegory" should be taken in a general rather than medieval sense, being a story in which the spiritual content is set forth in a concrete action and with characters whose movements are realistic but whose basic function is that of abstract symbols. Many have objected, however, that the film is composed of too many disparate elements: Bergman borrows freely from old frescoes he had seen as a child, which accounts for such allegorized sequences as Jof's vision of Mia in the traditional rose garden of the Virgin Mary, and Death sawing off the tree (of life) in which Skat, the actor, has taken refuge. Also, the idea of the chess game stems from medieval allegories. But the central characters fall outside such a pattern and cannot be classified according to any traditional symbolism.

Philosophically, *The Seventh Seal* departs from medieval allegory in two respects: the metaphysical uncertainty that characterizes Bergman's film has little in common with the *a priori* assumption of an orderly universe, which underlies original allegory; and the central character in the prototypal allegory is not haunted by doubt; his problem is his forgetfulness of God, and God emerges not as an enigma but as a father figure anxious to reach and save His straying child.

The philosophical mood of *The Seventh Seal* is related to the existentialist view that a human life is decided not in intellectual questioning but in the choice of action. To Jöns, the squire, who in spite of his cynical verbosity is compassionate in his deeds, the Knight is a fool who has wasted ten years of his life asking futile questions: "Ten years we sat in the Holy Land and let the snakes bite us, insects prick us, wild animals nip us, heathens slaughter us, the wine poison us, women give us lice, fleas feed on us, and fevers consume us, all to the glory of God. I'll tell you, our Crusade was so stupid that only a real idealist could have thought it up."

Jöns uses the term "idealist" in its original sense, i.e., a *man of ideas,* an intellectual. The Crusade was bound to be meaningless because Antonius Block kept looking *beyond* it for some intellectual truth; he was not committed to the pilgrimage as a living act but to his own rational mind, which demanded that God show Himself in divine essence: "I want knowledge, not faith, not suppositions, but knowledge. I want God to stretch out his hand toward me, reveal Himself and speak to me." God as object should make the Crusade a meaningful act.

The Crusader's search was also destined to be blasphemous, for as in the archetypal legend of the Fall, a desire for ultimate knowledge is treason against God. Bergman has grasped the paradoxical implications of the old myth: man cannot seek full intellectual cognizance of God without disobeying Him; the more he tries to understand the nature of God the further he removes himself from God. Bergman illustrates this gradual alienation of man from the divine by depicting in the Crusader a human being at first engaged in a holy enterprise but in the end willing to sell his soul to the Devil—could he only find him! For the Devil, the knight argues with insane logic, must know God since he only exists in his opposition to God.

In the most brutal scene in the film, staged as a kind of exorcism, the Crusader speaks to Tyan, who is about to be burnt as a witch:

Knight: They say that you have been in league with the Devil.

Tyan: Why do you ask?

Knight: Not out of curiosity, but for very personal reasons. I too want to meet him.

Tyan: Why?

Knight: I want to ask him about God. He, if anyone, must know.

Tyan: You can see him any time.

But to the Crusader the Devil as objectified reality remains as invisible and silent as God. Yet, Antonius Block fails to accept the implication that transcendental truth dwells in man himself, as potentialities of good and evil. Instead he tells Tyan: "I believe at times that to ask questions is the most important thing." The search has become his *raison d'être*.

Bergman juxtaposes the knight's intellectual probing and his relationship with Jof and Mia, the visionary artist and the maternal woman, whose son one day will "perform the impossible trick of making a ball stand still in the air" (i.e., like Christ he will transcend nature). The traditional function of the Crusader in medieval art was not as the colonizer of the Holy Land but as the protector of the Holy Family. Bergman's knight performs the same service. But in saving Jof and his family by distracting Death's attention away from them, Antonius Block loses the game—and his life. It is a situation of ironic blasphemy: Man redeems Christ. On the other hand, it is an act made possible only because the Crusader has caught a glimpse of love in his relationship with Jof and Mia. Perhaps the most crucial sequence in the film (and one that anticipates *Wild Strawberries*) is a low-keyed scene played on a sunny hillside, an idyllic picture of the knight as he is being offered milk and wild strawberries by Mia. Strawberries are sometimes associated with the Virgin in late Northern iconography, but milk and wild strawberries are also private symbols in Bergman's world, the Eucharist in a communion between human beings.

It is on this occasion that the knight vows: "I shall remember this moment. . . . I'll carry this memory between my hands as carefully as if it were a bowl filled to the brim with fresh milk. (*He turns his face away and looks out toward the sea and the colorless gray sky.*) And it will be an adequate sign—it will be enough for me."

But the Crusader does not keep his vow for long. The riddle of God continues to haunt him, and he is compelled to go on with his questioning. At one time it has brought about his fall from "paradise," his self-expulsion from a happy marriage. Antonius Block tells Mia of this loss of innocence: "We [my wife and I] were newly married and we played together. We laughed a great deal. I wrote songs to her eyes, to her nose, to her beautiful little ears. We went hunting together and at night we danced. The house was full of life."

The horribly negative aspect of the Crusader's search becomes evident in the final sequence of the film, when Antonius Block is reunited with his wife. It is a strangely cold and detached meeting. The wife, whom we see for the first time, is cast as a woman of ascetic features. Later she officiates at a last supper, during which every sacramental element of redemption is absent and only the mood of impending doom prevails. As Death knocks at the castle door, the wife intones the words from the Book of Revelations.

The film does not end, however, on this pessimistic note but reiterates the permanent counterpoint of the story, which is a tension between those who willingly or by force succumb to death, and those who survive, representing the eternal values in life: compassion and generous love. This tension finds its resolution in the final scene: Jof, Mia, and the child look toward the horizon where Jof sees all the other main characters who, led by Death, dance away to the country of shadows.

The figure of Death stands only on the threshold of the unknown; he is not a messenger, but merely a blind instrument. But he might be considered the focal point in the film. Like *Wood Painting, The Seventh Seal* concerns man's reactions in the face of eschatological matters. Almost all the characters can be linked to Death and evaluated according to his influence over them. While Skat and Raval live as though Death did not exist, and Tyan and the flagellants as though nothing else existed, the knight and Jöns carry on a resentful and challenging dialogue with Death. Although Jöns does not see the knight's opponent in the chess game until the end, he is preoccupied with the thought of death; he is horrified by it and mocks it, but he is never indifferent to it. Throughout the film he is confronted with signs of Death's power. As he rides along in the morning, singing a bawdy song, he catches sight of a huddled figure on the ground. Turning it over, he stares at a skull. Later on he discusses the death motif with the church painter, and in spite of his own nonchalance ("This is squire Jöns. He grins at Death. . . .") he is so sickened by the pictures that he has to ask for a brandy. Jöns loves life; he is angered by the thought of annihilation, and his last words as he faces Death are words of remonstrance: "I shall be silent, but under protest."

Jöns is more than the hedonist he appears to be. Like Antonius Block he represents the consciousness of modern man. The knight and his squire complement each other, and depict the skeptic personality facing a world where God is silent: one in futile introspection,

the other in gallant action. They do not offer an alternative. All
the film seems to say is that some people can live without illusions
and still function as useful social beings, while others succumb to
their need to believe and lose themselves in a search for God. At
one point the knight cries out: "Why can't I kill God within me?
Why does He live on in this painful and humiliating way even
though I curse Him and want to tear Him out of my heart? Why,
in spite of everything, is He a baffling reality that I can't shake off?"
In this statement we sense again the modern temper of *The Seventh
Seal*: the realization that moral will has given way to psychological
needs—which excludes a possibility of choice. Yet, both the knight
and Jöns are conceived as moral agents, and in this ambivalence
Bergman again establishes his affinity with existentialist philosophy
and its tenet that we must live as though we had a free will. The
insoluble dilemma dramatized in the fate of Antonius Block also
points to one of Ibsen's central themes: the curse (i.e., the moral judgment) that falls upon a man who *must* follow his calling.

There are several possible literary prototypes for *The Seventh
Seal*. Bergman himself has mentioned George Bernanos' *The Diary
of a Country Priest* as a source of inspiration. He also seems to
have had the Faust figure in mind, both as it appeared in the stage
version of *Ur-Faust* that Bergman produced at the Malmö City
Theater shortly before he began to work on *The Seventh Seal*, and
in Thomas Mann's *Dr. Faustus*, which had made a deep impression
on him. Strindberg also lent his voice to the film. His historical play
The Saga of the Folkungs (Folkungasagan) has a similar "cinematic"
form: a panoramic setting, swift changes of scenes, abrupt "cuts"
from mass scenes to intimate "close-ups." A train of flagellants appears in both works as well as quotations from the Revelation of St.
John the Divine (in Strindberg from the sixth chapter, in Bergman
from the eighth).

With his fondness for musical analogies, Bergman has referred to
The Seventh Seal as an oratorio. The comparison is suggestive but
misleading if taken too literally. An oratorio is usually performed
without action, costume, or scenery. Bergman's film is full of visual
splendor, and it has an excellent story. Furthermore, an oratorio is,
as a rule, not only based upon a religious theme but is anchored in
an unshaken faith in God and sung to his praise. *The Seventh Seal*,
on the other hand, progresses in a mood of religious ambivalence.
But no doubt Bergman never intended his "oratorio" to have more

than a certain structural similarity to the musical genre: a composition for solo voices, chorus, and orchestra.

If one were to look for an analogy to *The Seventh Seal* in another art form, it might be more accurate to describe it as a cinematic tapestry, on which are interwoven the fates of many people, and where symbolic details sometimes confuse but always intrigue the spectator, the total effect being one of great plastic clarity.

While the visual impact of *The Seventh Seal* is tremendous, the film is marred by occasional verbal awkwardness, less noticeable in the English version which avoids the rhetorical resonance of some of the dialogue and translates the knight's speech into colloquial language.

In *The Seventh Seal* movement is reserved for scenes that are visually descriptive, but spoken, introspective moments are not reflected by movement on the screen. This is in line with dramatic tradition: a Shakespearean soliloquy, for instance, is a physical pause. But Shakespeare's language possesses a visual power in itself, which Bergman's abstracted and prosaic language does not have. In later films Bergman develops—perhaps under the influence of TV—the close-up as an alternative to movement; the sensitive face of an actor or actress must then convey the feelings that the words alone cannot transmit.

As a film, *The Seventh Seal* can be placed in the mainstream of Swedish cinematic tradition. Abroad it has often been mentioned together with Carl Dreyer's *Day of Wrath*, but visually *The Seventh Seal* has little in common with this film. Dreyer's style is stark and realistic, his rhythm slow and heavy. By comparison Bergman appears volatile and a little eclectic; his style oscillates between realistic scene-painting and abstracted symbolism, and aligns him with Victor Sjöström and classical Swedish films like *Terje Vigen* (1916) and *The Phantom Carriage* (1921). Like Sjöström, Bergman has gradually realized that the cinema can be a medium that lends itself to introspection and analysis with more flexibility than the theater.

As Bergman began to internalize earlier social and parental problems and transform them into questions of personal identity and/or faith—a development which no doubt has been crucial in shaping *la nouvelle vague* in the French cinema—the environment lost its autonomous quality of nature lyricism or realistic backdrop. In Bergman's early works, a human being may identify himself with the landscape, but nature still exists as an objective reality, possessing powers of its own. In *The Seventh Seal* scenery and weather (a night in the forest, a strong wind) are used as ill omens, much the same as the dark clouds were used in *Illicit Interlude* to foreshadow the death of Henrik. In these instances the landscape serves as the artist's tool—one might call it Bergman's "Gothic quality."

But the landscape in *The Seventh Seal* is not only a ghostlike instrument; it emerges as a reflection of a state of mind, a metaphor of the self. The desolate landscape in the opening scenes of the film is an image of the isolation and despair of the knight. The landscape which appears in Isak Borg's dreams in *Wild Strawberries* is a logical consequence of this tendency—a heritage from Victor Sjöström—to treat the surroundings as subjective image.

Ingmar Bergman: The Middle Period
by PETER COWIE

Bergman is apparently fond of quoting Eugene O'Neill's claim that all dramatic art is worthless unless it deals with man's relationship to God. For Bergman, there has to be some power in the universe (he calls it God for want of a better word), a power that influences man's mind and situation. He is interested in this God because he feels Him, more than social and economic conditions, to be responsible for all the complexes, vanities, and desires that man is heir to, and which reduce him to a posturing idiot—to a Vogler, an Egerman, or an Ester. The principal characters in *The Seventh Seal (Det sjunde inseglet,* 1957) embody these traits. The film is set in the Middle Ages so that the figures can become more clearly defined, and so that their symbolic virtues and demerits can be stressed without bathos. It is an expansion of a one-act play called *Wood Painting (Trämålning,* 1954). "Inside the church," Bergman wrote in an introduction to this morality, "in the southern part of Småland, you can see our play, painted on the wall. It is just to the right as you go through the porch. The picture dates from the fourteenth century and its theme has been derived from impressions of a plague that was raging at that time, there and in the countryside round about." The play lacks the visual poetry of the film and can never provoke in one such a powerful feeling of involvement.

Following the example of Lindström and Sjöberg in *The Road to Heaven,* Bergman brings to life the peasant paintings in the Swedish churches. He recalls his study of the frescoes when as a child he used to accompany his father from one parish to another on a Sunday: "There was everything that one's imagination could desire—angels,

From Sweden 2 *by Peter Cowie (London: The Tantivy Press, in association with A. Zwemmer Ltd.; Cranbury, N. J.: A. S. Barnes & Co., 1970), pp. 142–51. Copyright © 1970 by Peter Cowie. Reprinted by permission of the author.*

saints, dragons, prophets, devils, human beings. All this surrounded by a heavenly, earthly and subterranean landscape of a strange yet familiar beauty. In a wood sat Death, playing chess with the Crusader. Clutching the branch of a tree was a naked man with staring eyes, while down below stood Death, sawing away to his heart's content. . . ." It is to Bergman's credit that these symbolic figures can still disturb in an age when the influence of the church is at its lowest ebb. The latent power of *The Seventh Seal* stems from an ever-present fear in man's mind; a fear of the unknown. That twentieth-century man lives in the shadow of nuclear catastrophe is not fundamental to the film; but it allows one to share the bewilderment of the knight and his companions. It is this search for knowledge that illuminates all Bergman's mature films. It imposes a pattern on life, which becomes a journey through time and space. The transience of human existence does not depress Bergman so much as the pitiful groping of man to comprehend the world around him.

The Seventh Seal, like *Wild Strawberries, The Face,* and *The Virgin Spring,* ends on a note of optimism, with the Holy Family leading their wagon along the sunlit shore. And to a certain extent the book of Revelation, where the title of the film originates, is for all its violent imagery, a song of consolation. "And they shall see his face; and his name shall be in their foreheads. And there shall be no night there; and they need no candle, neither light of the sun; for the Lord God giveth them light: and they shall reign for ever and ever" (Revelation 22:4–5). The opening of the seals provides an interval for man to consider his significance on earth. He must realize that he cannot overcome his fear or improve the world unless he chooses the most difficult path. Thus the knight plays chess with Death, risking his entire being for the hope of committing one worthy act before the Apocalypse. Bergman shows that he loses his right to choice of action if he falls under the influence of the church, whose only representatives in the film are Death disguised as a pastor, and a monk who screams at a band of flagellants as they pause in the village. The church is revered in the Middle Ages, while art, epitomized in the trio of wandering players, is ridiculed. "People here aren't interested in art," says Jof to his horse, and later in the film he is forced to perform like a bear in front of a sadistic crowd, the word "actor" hurled at him in abuse. The entertainer, as one has noted apropos of *Sawdust and Tinsel*

[*The Naked Night*], is always the object of contempt in Bergman's
world, and yet he possesses an innate comprehension of human
foibles and graces. Because he thinks in simple terms and plays on
basic emotions he clarifies by his work the darkest recesses of the
soul. But people do not like to know the truth and grow angry
when they see themselves reflected in art, as Jöns mentions to the
church painter. In Bergman's eyes, this relationship between the
performer and his public corresponds closely to the antagonism
between the dogmatist and the heretic in the Middle Ages, between
those who believe in the doctrines of the church and those who
question its authority.

The Knight has been made skeptical by events. One learns that
he had been persuaded by Raval to leave on a Crusade a decade
earlier. He has sought for God and encountered only a concept.
"Is it so hard to conceive of God with the senses?" he asks at the
confessional. "How can we have faith in those who believe when
we can't have faith in ourselves? What is going to happen to those
of us who want to believe but cannot? And what is to become of
those who neither want to nor are capable of believing?"—words
of despair and disenchantment that will be echoed by Tomas in
Winter Light. But Block is still sure that life must evince some
significance. He is an acutely sensitive man and this is why—
allegorically—he alone (save the visionary Jof) can see Death and
delay the Apocalypse. When he flexes his hand in the chapel after
being deceived by Death, the action becomes a stirring symbol of
the will-to-live in man, which has been the source of human love
and ideals. "This is my hand," he says ardently, "I can move it,
feel the blood pulsing through it. The Sun is still high in the sky
and I, Antonius Block, am playing chess with Death." He is moved
by the simple innocence of Jof and Mia when he meets them on the
hillside while waiting for Death to resume the match. He begins to
sense that this family (surely the scriptural connotations of their
names are not accidental) must be shielded from the fear of Death.
If he can translate his ideals into an effective gesture he can die
without regrets. Mia prepares a bowl of fresh milk and some strawberries, that recurrent Bergman token of passing happiness. The
peace of the scene enervates the knight (as the lunch on the terrace
in *Wild Strawberries* prompts Isak to express his true feelings).
Wistfully, he thinks of his wife whom he has not seen for ten years,
and then describes his doubts with unerring lucidity. "Faith is like

loving someone who is out there in the darkness but never appears, however loudly you call." The serenity and poignance of this scene above the sea is most perfectly captured, however, in the knight's subsequent reflection: "I shall remember this moment, the silence, the twilight, the bowl of strawberries and milk, your faces in the dusk, Mikael sleeping, Jof with his lyre. I'll carry this memory between my hands as carefully as if it were a bowl filled with fresh milk. It will be a sign—and a great consolation." Life does after all afford the occasional charmed moment, and this tenderly-wrought sequence is unsurpassed in the Swedish cinema in its combination of plastic beauty and lyrical monologue. . . .

The knight has his *alter ego* in the squire, Jöns . . . despite the profoundly individual qualities of the two men. Jöns waits always at his back with his cynicism and captious remarks. Block's conscious mind refuses to acknowledge the intelligence of the squire's attitude. As they stand, side by side, watching a witch being burned at the stake, the knight clenches his teeth and cries, "There must be something!" while Jöns comments drily, "Look at her eyes, my lord. Her poor brain has just made a discovery—emptiness . . . we see what she sees and her terror is ours." And although Block shakes his head vigorously at the squire's assertion, it is obvious that he has become aware emotionally of what previously he had suspected intellectually—that man must rely solely on himself to counter Death. He joins forces with the modern Swedish philosopher, Hedenius, in believing that religious experience must be capable of communication even to a nonbeliever.

When Block reaches his castle after the long night's march the anxiety has ebbed from him. He has allowed Jof and Mia to escape by sweeping the chessmen off the board at the very climax of the game with Death. His wife Karin is alone in the castle. "Somewhere in your eyes, somewhere in your face," she says, "is the boy who went away so many years ago." "It's over now, and I'm a little tired," replies Block. One can almost feel the melancholy and resignation that steals over him. Death is no longer an adversary: he is a minister of eternal rest. Block prays dutifully to the last, but he has been fortified by the encounter with Jof and Mia, the only meaningful incident in a life that has appeared ridiculous in its juxtaposition of suffering and sterility, cruelty and perplexity. The knight is Bergman's supreme Faust figure, grappling with Death in a vain attempt to reconcile the contradictions inherent in life. One responds in the affirmative to Marcel Martin's question: "Are the tormented Christians that Bergman depicts in all his films tormented because they are bad Christians or rather because they are simply poor men who do not find in religion either comfort in their misery or the solution to their problems?" [1]

For some critics, including Jörn Donner, Jöns is the most interesting character in the film. One perhaps identifies with his pragmatic hedonism more readily than one does with the intellectual anguish of the knight. He scowls at his master behind his back, but he is quick to remedy injustice and to brand a villain like Raval. The events of the day affect him severely. As he rides along the hills, he dismounts to ask the way of a man seated beside the path. He is a corpse in a black cowl. This is the first shock for the squire. He tells Block that the man was "most eloquent"—doubly ironic, for the sight brings home to Jöns the ravages of the plague. Where Block is ascetic and humourless, Jöns is lecherous and sardonic; where Block is unconcerned with the physical details of the plague, Jöns is troubled more than he cares to admit by the hideous paintings on the chapel walls. He asks for brandy to blind him to this horror, and paints a caricature of himself. "This is squire Jöns. He grins at Death, mocks the Lord, laughs at himself and leers at the girls. His world is a Jöns-world, believable only to himself, ridiculous to all including himself, meaningless to heaven and of no interest to hell." At the end, confronted with Death in the castle, he urges his master to "feel to the very end the triumph of being alive." Jöns is more akin than Block to modern man. The teachings of the church fill him with disgust and scorn. ("Our Crusade was so stupid that only a genuine idealist could have thought it up.") He is moved by bestiality but convinced that he cannot improve the world. "Love is the blackest of all plagues, but you don't die of it," he says. He lacks the vision to distinguish between the saintly and the helpless. He saves the girl from being raped by Raval, but he leads her only to Death. He cannot see Death. His life hinges on compromise rather than aspiration. It is Jöns, with his jovial words of advice and his readiness to assist, who helps his friends and himself to come to terms with the misery of existence, but it is the knight who dies in an attempt to change the situation.

Jöns and the other characters in *The Seventh Seal* present the

---

[1] Martin, Marcel. Review of *Le Silence,* in *Cinéma 64* (Paris: May 1964).

knight with pointers towards a different attitude to life. "Blessed
are the pure in heart, for they shall see God," is the most apposite
description of Jof and Mia. They are simple folk who escape Death
in the end because they never question God's existence or love. "One
day is like another," says Mia. "The summer, of course, is better
than the winter, because in summer you don't have to be cold. But
spring is best of all." Theirs is an implicit faith in the beauty of
life which relates them to other Bergman characters such as Sara in
Wild Strawberries and Simson in *The Face*. Jof is a visionary who
suddenly sees the Virgin walking sedately across a lawn with her
child (an incident inspired, Bergman has admitted, by George
Bernanos's descriptions in *The Diary of a Country Priest*), and
later perceives Death playing chess with the knight. He also dreams
that his baby son Mikael will be a great juggler and perform the
one impossible trick—to make a ball stand still in the air. Jean
D'Yvoire, in a study of the film's metaphysical values, claims that
"the trick in question symbolizes the interruption of cosmic movement, in other words the end of the world, the return to stability
through reabsorption in the principle of Being: one more way of
suggesting the comparison of the child with the saviour of the
world, the only one capable of effecting this reintegration in the
immobility of God." [2]

The love that binds Jof and Mia is stronger than the menace of
Death. When in the morning sunshine, Mia tells Jof to stop
juggling and says, smiling, "I love you," the words are so tender
and sincere that Death is no more than an empty mask dangling
beside the caravan. One has to return to *Summer Interlude* to find
such an enchanting picture of human affection; and Jof and Mia
are more eternal creatures than Henrik and Marie. Their love
remains intact at the end of the film; they are the faultless souls
who survive to start a train of hope for humanity again. Bergman
has said, "Whenever I am in doubt or uncertainty I take refuge
in the vision of a simple and pure love. I find this love in those
spontaneous women who . . . are the incarnation of purity." [3]

Jof is essentially a clown. Bergman feels that the clown can con-
tribute to his investigation into man's predicament. Moments of

[2] Fovez, Elie, Ayfre, Amédée, and D'Yvoire, Jean. *"Le Septième Sceau." Télé-
ciné* (Paris: August–September 1958).

[3] Burvenich, Jos. *Thèmes d'Inspiration d'Ingmar Bergman*. Brussels: Club du
Livre de Cinéma, March 1960.

frivolity are often set beside moments of terror so that it becomes difficult to disentangle jest from threat. When Jof and Mia sing and dance at the village they are interrupted by the arrival of a group of flagellants. While their gaiety turns to dread, Skat, dressed as Pan, has sidled away lecherously behind some bushes with the giggling wife of the local blacksmith Plog. A short time afterwards Jof is taunted by Plog and Raval at the inn. Not until the last moment does he grasp the gravity of his situation. He responds pertly and innocently in the silence. Fear only assails him when he is made to dance like a bear on the table and his audience, so minatory before, giggles hysterically. Skat and Plog both have the familiar qualities of the puppet-show villain; their querulous exchanges and mannered gestures—suave on the one hand, lumbering on the other—become virtually an art in themselves. Their antics offset the severity of the remainder of the film like the porters in *Macbeth* and the gravediggers in *Hamlet*. Skat enjoys his fleeting hour of dirty love with the smith's wife, but he is trapped by Death in the midst of his self-congratulation. His vanity betrays him. Plog is enraged when his little Lisa runs off with this "perfumed slob," but he has admitted in his earlier conversation with Jöns that he is sick to death of marriage. "Women's nagging, the shrieking of children and wet nappies, sharp nails and sharp words, blows and pokes, and the devil's aunt for a mother-in-law." He is enmeshed, like Albert in *Sawdust and Tinsel*, in his dissatisfaction, his fear of loneliness prevailing over his disapproval of Lisa.

Raval is yet another in the long line of repugnant ecclesiastics in Bergman's world. Jöns finds him robbing a dead man and ready to rape a serving-girl. Raval—"Doctor Mirabilis, Coelestis et Diabolis" as the squire calls him sarcastically—had urged the knight to leave on the Crusade, so that he and his accomplices could indulge their thieving instincts. He is active, malicious evidence of the unethical advantage the ministers of the church took of most men's naïveté in the Middle Ages. It is quite appropriate that he should be later struck down by the plague which he regards as an instrument of divine disfavor. When he emerges from the forest, he grovels before Jöns and his girl in a last servile plea for water. He, the dispenser of God's word, is the most anxious to escape Death, whose clean, withdrawn honesty is preferable to the sadistic behavior of this seminarist.

The young girl condemned as a witch is first seen when Block and Jöns leave the chapel. She is tied to a stake. Men-at-arms are on guard, legs flung wide in oppressive stance. A tight-lipped monk mutters prayers over her. She has been found having "carnal intercourse with the Evil One," and is burned in the evening. Before she dies, she is questioned by the knight. "I too want to meet the Devil," he tells her, "I want to ask him about God. He, if anyone, must know." But the girl has been convinced by the priests that the Devil is within her. She does not need, as Block does, oracular proof. She is a victim of the church, a victim of intolerance, and the despair that lights her eyes as the flames and smoke swirl about her is repugnant to Jöns and to the knight. For if at the moment of death there is no revelation, surely there is no purpose in life?

Perhaps the most intriguing aspect of *The Seventh Seal* is the way Bergman creates an atmosphere in which these afflicted people can perform so persuasively. The film begins on a rocky beach, which is viewed from a lofty angle as the knight awakes with the dawn. There is a marked feeling of desolation and all extraneous sounds are absent from the encounter with Death, giving it an unearthly quality as the landscape darkens. After the initial moves in the game of chess, the knight and his squire ride along the ridge overlooking the sea. Bergman uses a series of dissolves so that the images disintegrate in glaucous sunlight, and the heat becomes almost palpable, as it does in the flashback at the beginning of *Sawdust and Tinsel*. But while the sea summons up resonances of hope, of arrival and departure, the chapel where the Crusaders stop briefly has the aura of a prison. Abstract concepts are translated into hard, tangible symbols throughout *The Seventh Seal,* and the grille that separates Block from his opponent in the confessional bars the knight's progress towards knowledge. In the porch, "Jöns watches the painter at work on his frescoes. From now onwards the dramatic highpoints of the film are derived more closely from such mural paintings. The band of flagellants that appears in the next village fulfill the painter's description when he talks to Jöns. "Mobs of people who call themselves Slaves of Sin are swarming over the country, flagellating themselves and others, all for the Glory of God." The smoke from the censers, the skulls carried aloft, the cross with its ascetic Christ-effigy, the half-naked penitents who lash each other's backs with spasmodic, jerking movements, all fuse into an appalling vision, worthy of Hieronymous Bosch. As the procession enters the square, Bergman shoots the scene from a series of low camera angles, so as to suggest the terror that these wretches inspire in the onlookers; but when they have been harangued by a monk and stumble on their way again, the high camera set-ups reduce them to insignificance. Their wailing dies away and by a cunning dissolve Bergman creates the impression that they have disappeared into the barren ground, symbolizing the futility of their religious fervor.

The burning of the witch is also a familiar feature of medieval frescoes. This takes place in the depths of the forest, which has closed round the knight and his companions as night falls, in sharp contrast to the open horizons of the sea that lighten the scene with the strawberries and the milk during the afternoon. Death follows invisibly, except when he claims Skat, and sits disguised as a monk near the stake. He glides into the frame from one side or another, always unexpected. The most famous mural image of all is reserved for the concluding sequence. Jof sees the victims dancing away in the grey dawn, clinging to one another in the line *Totentanz,* while "the rain washes their faces and cleans the salt of the tears from their cheeks." This is almost a direct quotation from Revelation 7. Bergman's technical achievement lies in his giving visual drama to these Biblical texts. Even the lightning and the winds that descend on the forest are an exact representation of the elemental forces unleased in Revelation 7:5.

The Seventh Seal, like the moralities, is built on stylization. The characters wear their sentiments on their sleeve. The overriding symbol, Death himself, appears like a motif at a number of crucial psychological stages in the film, culminating in his terrifying confession of ignorance to the knight after he has defeated him in the game of chess. Hope becomes a squirrel bounding on to a tree stump after Skat's death, or a ray of moonlight filling a forest glade as Raval lies dead, or a caravan with its errant, innocent owners trundling along the seashore into the sun. Disillusion becomes the rigid gaze of a girl on the stake; resignation, the tossing of a log on a fire by a listless, lonely wife; horror, the rhythmical banging of beer mugs on an inn table while a man dances for his life. It is this triumphant blend of literary antecedent and visual metaphor that makes *The Seventh Seal* such a profound and ambitious film, unequalled in the Swedish cinema as an exercise in tempered expressionism, less ornate than *Sawdust and Tinsel,* less theatrical than *Miss Julie.* Its theme is universal and yet particularly momentous to the Swedes; the fundamental situation of men faced by death and striving to find some meaning in life is common to the work of Strindberg and Lagerkvist. At this stage Bergman neither denies nor affirms Christian tradition. He probes, he interrogates.

Ingmar's Ansikte

by M. MARTINEZ CARRIL

Recently with *The Seventh Seal,* Bergman dares to tackle head-on a spiritual theme. In the middle of the fourteenth century a knight and his squire arrive in Sweden, returning from the Crusades. The knight meets Death (Bengt Ekerot, his face asexual) and challenges him to a game of chess. The knight and squire make their way through the countryside, devastated by the plague, to the knight's estate where von Sydow's wife (Inga Landgré) is waiting. That itenerary is intersected by others: a pair of comedians who live in harmony (Nils Poppe, Bibi Andersson), a procession of flagellants, a presumed witch (Maud Hanson) who is being led to the stake. Finally in the last scenes, the two paths are juxtaposed: the one undertaken by Death with those whom Death has overtaken, in a phantasmagoric dance on the line of the distant horizon; and the other path that of the pair of comedians with their little son, safe and moving toward a new life, a paraphrase of the new life that was born with Jesus.

In *The Naked Night,* the members of a troupe arrived in a provincial city, suffered there various crises, and then continued their journey. In *Dreams* the two female protagonists start a journey in a train, which can be seen as an escape, like the beginning of an interior trip. In *Wild Strawberries* the elderly Professor Borg undertakes an anxious journey during which he faces his own questions. The women in *The Silence* arrive by train to a mysterious city and one of them begins her return in the last scenes. And all four of the characters in *Through a Glass Darkly* seem to emerge from the horizon in a movement opposite that of the final scene in *The Seventh Seal.* Also in *Thirst, Illicit Interlude,* and *Summer with*

From Cuadernos de Cine Club del Uruguay, *Montevideo, 1965. Reprinted by permission of Cine Club del Uruguay. Translated from the Spanish by Harriet Goldberg.*

Monica, the male and female protagonists of Bergman's films travel from one place to another as if that physical movement were a departure to new and more intimate anxieties, which are visualized through the physical action. But in few instances has he exploited this device as much as in *The Seventh Seal.*

The whole film is conceived along a line of existentialist thought, which is not alien to Bergman's earlier and later works. But it is no longer a question of reducing into dramatic terms someone else's hell. The film deals with a sense of life, but from a metaphysical perspective rather than a psychological or dramatic one. Even though he does not admit it clearly, the knight Antonius Block suggests that "to feel anguish is an adventure through which all men must pass if they do not want to be led to perdition" (according to Kierkegaard). If life is not justified except as a function of that anguish, its questions—faced equally by Death, the witch, Block himself, and the squire—don't lead to nihilism but rather to an ambiguous and disconcerting affirmation. Death reveals the possibilities of real life. Because of this the apparent sacrifice of the knight is not futile. The film ends with an affirmation of life, with the pair of comedians and with the little Mikael (perhaps the archangel Michael) already far away from Death.

In this way the metaphysical question that spurs on the knight and his squire (not the other characters, which confirms that the two of them are different aspects of one being) reaches the spectator emotionally through the creation of special surroundings where light disappears from the first scene (once Death has presented himself to the knight), where the external signs of death keep following each other with a growing rhythm (beginning with a man whose face is eaten away and ending with the procession of flagellants), where at last there is a strong link between the unreal (the visions of Jof which allude to the unknown and to the future) and the concrete and tangible (all the realistic and direct adaptations of the Nordic Middle Ages). Through its setting in historical time the film converts itself into a timeless allegory where the Biblical text seems to refer both to atomic destruction and to the Book of Revelations ("And when he had opened the seventh Seal, there was silence about the space of half an hour"). Through this approach, the route (the various routes that intercept one another) acquires a clean symbolic sense. Life seems to stop during the duration of the film while the characters seek an answer.

The Religious Scope of
THE SEVENTH SEAL
by AMEDÉE AYFRE

To point out the religious significance of this work, it would doubtless be necessary to begin with Bergman's title, whose importance cannot be emphasized too much. The author lived in a milieu too impregnated with Biblical culture for us to believe that he chose an exact word from the Apocalypse by chance or because of its mysterious or evocative flavor.

To understand its full significance, one must refer to the text itself, chapter 5, verse 1, as the best commentators translate it. The book which, in Saint John's version, God holds in his right hand is depicted as a papyrus scroll and not as a bound codex. As a matter of fact, this fact alone explains how John can see what is written on the other side, which would not make sense with a codex, but which happened rather often with papyrus. Once these scrolls were rolled up, seals were put on one line along the exterior border of the sheet which was thus stuck to the roll. Such was, among other things, the arrangement required by Roman law for testaments. That is why one cannot begin reading these texts before breaking the seven seals.

The seventh seal is thus the last, the one whose rupture leads to the supreme revelation of the secrets contained in the Book of God. Only the Lamb, that is, according to the same Aramaic word, the Servant, which is Christ, can proceed to this Revelation and unseal

"Portée religieuse du Septième sceau" by Amedée Ayfre. From Télé-ciné, no. 77 (August–September 1958). Reprinted by permission of Télé-ciné, 24 boulevard Poissonière, Paris. Translated by Kristine Hughie and Birgitta Steene.

the Book. The scenes corresponding to the opening of each seal do not thus constitute a partial revelation of the contents of the book, but rather the symbol of these fundamental questions which mark man's condition and which make man ask the reason for his presence in the world. It is the mysterious horsemen—Power, Violence, Hunger, and Death—who escort man throughout all time and who cause all unjustly smitten innocents to ask at the fifth seal: how long, Lord, will evil be relentlessly triumphant? Is there really hope of judgment, a day of justice when, in the confusion of cosmic powers, masters of destiny (sixth seal), the sovereign mercy of God who "shall feed them and shall lead them unto fountains of waters: and . . . shall wipe away all tears from their eyes" will finally descend upon "a great multitude, which no man could number of all nations, and kindreds, and people, and tongues." (Revelation 7:9, 17).

This is the irrefutable question inspired by the plagues of War, Famine, and Pestilence, who are included in the supreme plague— Death—this is the question which the Book, posed in the open hand of God, must answer after the seventh seal is broken. Again, only the Lamb, the Servant, Master of Death, can do it because he has suffered death and has triumphed over it. . . .

"And when he had opened the seventh seal," the text tells us, "there was silence in heaven about the space of half an hour."

This impressive silence, magnificently evoked in the film by the Johannic eagle, immobile in the clouds, marks the supreme expectation of the Revelation while the Book of Secrets, now unsealed, slowly unrolls.

Bergman's whole film, one could say, takes place in a half hour. This is the delay that the knight, washed up on the shore, demands of Death. While the plagues continue to rage down here, he will have to try to search in the "silence in the sky" for the secret which it seems to him must reveal itself beyond the last broken seal.

But for Bergman this questioning will remain unanswered. The Book of Secrets may be unrolled, but no one knows if there is anything in it, in any case, no one could interpret it. Bergman remains on the threshold of the Apocalypse, on the threshold of the Revelation. "The question remains," he will tell us.

One realizes, appropriately, that atheists as well as Christians could not help but give a meaning to the question, each in their own way which served as their own answer. But the knight is not

to be identified with either the skeptical squire or the naive
mountebank. He travels with one, he meets the other. Both become
his "faithful companions."

One represents naive, spontaneous, *natural* belief which moves
at ease in a universe beyond sin. This is the childhood paradise
that the knight forfeited when he began to ask questions, but for
which he remains irreparably nostalgic. The other represents un-
belief, brutal negation, the refusal of illusions. He prefers the
ascertainment of an evil unaware of the good to the installation of
a good unaware of the evil. Instead of the woman who smiles with
love on a cot, he chooses—a reflection of his soul—the woman who
is mute with horror before the plagues of the world, and only waits
for everything to be consumed.

Between happiness and an equally calm despair, the knight continues to question himself. He wants to know. But the delay which
is allowed him can only lead him to two certainties. On one hand,
the childhood paradise is certainly lost for those who have once
left it. To want to return without the grace of innocence would
lead only to the ridiculous personage of the sensual, vulgar mountebank [Skat], a parasite of the happiness of some and of the un-
happiness of others, whose life—and death—seem hopelessly false.
He is the farcical picture of that other tragic parasite: the equivocal
and sordid defrocked monk who has become a grave-robber.

On the other hand, the end of the world—I mean its finite,
perishable, mortal character—forces itself on anyone who simply
opens his eyes. Man's world, where everyone insists—with courage,
despair, or unconsciousness—on prolonging a life already marked by
death, is entirely, secretly undermined by the same unchangeable
evil. The star called Wormwood is already at work contaminating
all the waters with her pestilential bitterness. The end of the world
is already there, inscribed in its very nature.

And it is not by beating oneself until one bleeds[1] or by torturing
or by burning at the stake bodies suspected of hiding the secret of
their evil that one will cut out this cancer. We will only end by
giving it new faces, because even if man can play with death, it is
not in his power to destroy it.

---

[1] We know that Pope Clement VI condemned the companies of Flagellants in
1349.

What will the knight do from then on between these two certainties of a paradise that is illusory for him, and a world which is too
marked by death for him to love it? The God of innocence is a lost
dream, but to replace it, to make the world divine would be at
least as false. Doubtless eternity is impossible, but time is certainly
finite. What do you do then, when you refuse to continue in the
reading of the Book, when you declare that there is nothing to be
found beside the altars or behind the gratings of the confessionals
but Death himself, always Death who knows nothing—what is there
to do but to follow Death to the end? Perhaps it is beyond this
macabre dance that the Secret is found which no one on this side
has been able to discover. Will it assume, even from afar and in a
strangely marvelous light, the figure of innocent and grave love
with which the film leaves us in the final shot? Perhaps. But this
"perhaps" remains very persuasive, not only due to affirmation but
to hope. This "perhaps" would be rather well defined by this
sentence found in another allegoric film, *Prison*: "What is to come
cannot be worse."

If to be a Christian means to affirm what the atheist denies, if to
be an atheist means to deny what the Christian affirms, Ingmar
Bergman is neither one nor the other. He neither affirms nor denies;
he asks without daring to hope for an answer to his question.

But does he know that his question is badly stated? The present
dilemma which he says he feels forced to express is perhaps less
serious than he thinks. Between the spontaneous, natural, naive faith
of the juggler and the brutal, lucid disbelief of the squire; between
the childish optimism of the heart and the adult pessimism of the
mind; between life lived joyously in the stream of Nature and the
instinct of death at work everywhere in an evil world, there is still
room, beyond belief and doubt, for a Faith without complaisance,
for a Faith, which, according to the words of St. Augustine, continues to search because it has already found; for a tragic optimism
which is not founded on hope but on a forgetfulness of Evil; for a
life which doubtless hides the seeds of death but also the promises
of resurrection.

It is true that to know this, it would have been necessary to
pursue to the end, well beyond the seventh seal, the reading of the
book of "Consolation," which is the Apocalypse. One would perhaps
have seen then that the vision of human time proposed to us

implies, in the heart of its unchanging finiteness, a mysterious presence of eternity which already *indicates* the meaning to us, waiting to reveal itself fully. So the servants of the Lamb "shall see his face, and his name will be in their foreheads. And there shall be no night there; and they need no candle, neither light of the sun; for the Lord God giveth them light: and they shall reign for ever and ever" (Revelation 2:4–5).

Ingmar Bergman Wants to Be the Kaj Munk of Sweden[1]

by IVAR HARRIE

Now at long last I have seen and heard Bergman's new film—
after having heard and read all the commotion about it.

And it turns out once again to prove just how difficult it is for a
person who is used to drama and fiction to understand the commotion around a *film* and perhaps, to a certain extent, pictorial art;
a person who of course has gone to the movies quite often during a
little more than forty years, but who has never succeeded in becoming one of the cinematically saved or initiated.

It has been said in the current discussion by a writer who is
eminently discerning in spite of occasional accidents to the contrary, that fiction is treated with "ridiculous seriousness" compared
to film. Quite the contrary, I dare ascertain. What is difficult to
comprehend in film discussions and film happenings—sometimes
having unintentional comic effects—is precisely the dead seriousness,
the solemn misuse of big words on both sides.

Certainly the cinema has produced great, dizzyingly great art—
but usually greatest when it has seized upon what it can present in
terms of naive fairy tale or amusing sport and when it has given
such entertaining an ironic double meaning. It is very rare that dead-
serious film becomes true art. Both the message and the presentation of the problem usually become popular editions in the bad
sense, caricaturelike and coarse simplifications.

"Ingmar Bergman vill vara Sveriges Kaj Munk" by *Ivar Harrie. From*
Expressen (*Stockholm*), *March 2, 1957. Reprinted by permission of the
author. Translated from the Swedish by Birgitta Steene.*

[1] [Kaj Munk was a Danish preacher and playwright assassinated by the Germans in 1944.]

If ever a film carries out a deeply serious theme without making it banal, without transcribing it to pulp jargon—as in the film version of Simenon's *The Snow Was Dirty*—the film critics immediately become irritated, confused, unmerciful.

DELIBERATELY FALSIFIED

Ingmar Bergman knows this since he is the Swedish poet who has found his natural and obvious medium in the film. Once he created a serious film where nothing was made trivial—*Woman without a Face*. He has made splendid numbers out of falsely naive film stories where in order to make a desperate surrealistic joke the resources of the film technician have been exploited: *The Naked Night, Secrets of Women,* and above all, *Smiles of a Summer Night*.

But now there has been a great deal of commotion around his very costly [!] mystery play *The Seventh Seal,* which has stunningly beautiful performances by a group of great actors and a wonderfully cooperative ensemble.

What is one to think of *The Seventh Seal?*

Well, naturally the performance is a key example of how problems are distorted and themes coarsened when a stage poem is translated into cinematic language.

In his little play *Wood Painting* Ingmar Bergman found, in the Dance of Death motif and the Black Death atmosphere, honest and clear expressions of the oscillation in our own time between fear of hell and a firm belief in salvation.

In the film the *leitmotifs* are made trivial, misused to serve as long-winded, pedantic object lessons. The original inspiration has been falsified—deliberately. For now it was a question of making a film, a film at any price, and a dead serious film, a "Biblia Pauperum," a pictorial bible for those poor in spirit.

POET OF IMAGES

Ingmar Bergman holds on to that intention stubbornly: hence the message of the film becomes pure rubbish and the actors are forced to deliver cues which do not reveal a genius but rather poor taste—as the creator of dialogue Ingmar Bergman must be the Swedish master of precious drivel.

But at the same time he is a great poet, a poet of images. And a film should be a poem—in this case a lyrical and sacral poem—in images. And in that respect his inspiration has not let him down; the pictorial power of the sequences is magnificent, in its highest moments catastrophic.

There is no cause for commotion with regard to Ingmar Bergman's new film. He is what he is—a very bad author, a very great director. A poet of the pictorial sequence, with an ability to get his actors to give of their very best in plastic mimicry to create the cinematic effect he has planned.

THE RETURN OF THE CLOWNS

Don't let us take him with "ridiculous seriousness." He wants to be an entertainer, a clown in the marketplace, and he wants to make his actors join him. He has saved his finest direction and personal instruction to the performance of the clowns and to the scene with the professional church painter.

But don't forget that he has projected himself into the role of the flagellants as well. The clown also wants to be a popular, a terribly popular preacher. He expresses himself with equal vulgarity in both parts—and with equal honesty. He has found that the film as an art form means both the return of the clowns and the return of the preaching mendicant friars.

His ambition is, in one word, to be Sweden's Kaj Munk. It is an ambition that might seem presumptuous. But Ingmar Bergman has the right to have it. It raises his role above the commotion.

Bergman the Poet
by HARRY SCHEIN

A short sequence in Ingmar Bergman's *The Seventh Seal* can, if analyzed really in depth, provide a useful illustration of some general views, not of the film, which, for natural reasons, I shall not review, but of Bergman's way of working.

In the sequence there are two roles: Death (Bengt Ekerot) and the actor (Erik Strandmark). The actor has just escaped a jealous smith by stabbing himself in the heart with a fake knife and has been left alone to die in the forest. The sequence can be assumed to start with the actor looking around cautiously. When discovering that he is alone he praises himself for his acting talent. But he is afraid of trolls and wild animals in the forest and decides to spend the night high up in a tree. Just as he is climbing the tree, the spectator discovers Death in the background. When the actor settles down on a branch, Death begins to saw off the trunk of the tree. The actor looks down with surprise at the back of the sawer, asking him snottily to leave his tree alone. Death looks up and says to the actor that his time is up. The actor recognizes Death and answers terrified: "I don't have time." The argument makes little impression. In utmost distress the actor now wonders if Death cannot make an exception. "Aren't there any special rules for actors?" he asks. Death denies this with an amused smile. A close-up of the actor's face shows us the sudden terror at the moment of death, followed immediately by a close-up of the cleavage in the falling tree with accompanying sound. Silence. Close-up of the stump of the tree. A squirrel jumps up on it, sniffing around for a while and disappears. End of sequence.

"Poeten Bergman" by Harry Schein. From BLM *26, no. 4 (April 1957): 350–53. Reprinted by permission of the author. Translated from the Swedish by Birgitta Steene.*

From this prosaic synopsis of a small and—from the point of view of the film—not very important sequence, a series of motifs, reminiscences and devices can be distinguished:

1. The basic motif—Death sawing off a tree in whose crown a human being is hiding—comes, according to Bergman, from a medieval painting in the church of Täby.
2. The dialogue is to a large extent taken from Bergman's own play *The Death of Punch.*
3. Drastic and shocking transition from burlesque comedy (the actor's fake suicide) to horror-filled drama (the appearance of Death).
4. Drastic and shocking transition from horror-filled drama (the moment of death) to public-appealing idyll (the squirrel).
5. Associatively tense transition from fake death to real death.
6. Mocking of histrionic vanity, which demands special privileges, even of Death.
7. Enamored admiration of the power of the theater to entice a little smile from Death, who is otherwise all serious.
8. Literary coquetry with the pun "your time is up—I don't have time."
9. Irrational but associatively strong dissolve with the squirrel, whose presence can neither be explained nor analyzed but only recognized as an essential coloration of the whole sequence.

Points 1 and 2 show us how ruthlessly Bergman steals, from himself and others. Points 3 and 4 show how Bergman wants to shock; he wants to put the spectators in an emotional state (which is characteristic of him also as a theater director) but not to direct their emotions in a precise, meaningful direction. Furthermore, points 3 and 4 give one of the keys to the film's composition, in which light and darkness, laughter and seriousness, comedy and drama succeed each other in a regular and logical rhythm. Points 6 and 7 give, through their very ambivalence, an impression of social realism in the only area where Bergman has enough interest, that is, in his relationship to the theater and its people. Through its sophisticated pretentiousness point 8 shows us Bergman as an ambitious but poor author. Points 5 and 9 show us Bergman as a poet, unfortunately not in my resume, of course, but quite convincingly in the film. And my whole analysis points out something uniquely characteristic for *The Seventh Seal*: almost every sequence in this film could be analyzed in a similar way, more or less independently of the film as a whole, something which is almost impossible to do in ordinary feature films.

Hence from this point of view *The Seventh Seal*, Ingmar Bergman's most important film to date, can be regarded as a filmic collection of stories. The fact that the film as a dramatic whole is exquisitely composed and balanced by a formal sensitivity that can only be described in musical terms does not prevent it from lacking thematic composition, a fully realized and coherent thought. It shows—and this is what is interesting—how it is possible to make a brilliant film not without having anything to say (Bergman has a lot to say) but without having anything clear and well-conceived to say.

The Stockholm critics received the film with an outburst of inarticulate praise.

Ingmar Bergman writes and directs for the theater and the film. In these four occupations he makes use of *technically* different means of expression for the same needs of expression, for the same conception. One has to accept him for what he is. To his personality belong, among other things, a good portion of sentimentality, literary presumption, a certain lack of moral integrity, a demonstrative indifference to all social contexts outside sex and the theater. To his personality belong also a somnambular intuition for dramatic effect, a poetically irrational boldness, a ruthless exploitation of ideas and motifs even though they might be totally foreign to him in their origin. His personality includes an egocentricity that makes it possible for him to lend an exaggerated central importance to minute points in the development of his character. And finally Bergman has a purely practical ability to adjust and an opportunely mocking self-irony that takes the edge out of the kind of demonic madness which sometimes—as in the case of Strindberg—can be conveyed through the very force of rabidness. And finally Bergman possesses a brilliant craftsmanship in the theater and the film. All of this is Ingmar Bergman. With these resources and this lack of resources he influences his public, even the qualified public. He plays with them, makes them happy, frightens them; he employs *any* means as long as they are effective, in any direction as long as there is a stir.

Ingmar Bergman's genius is not narrative, hardly even pictorial; it is transforming. In a discussion some time ago Lars-Erik Kjellgren

challenged the film-aesthetic subtleties of the twenties and thirties.
To him film is simply a white screen waiting to be filled. And Bergman fills it more than most. If one really takes joy in the cheap and
quite irrelevant malice of recognition, one might say that with
The Seventh Seal Bergman fills the screen with a series of anach-
ronisms, with noble pastiche, with Strindberg's *The Saga of the
Folkungs,* with Dreyer's *Day of Wrath,* with the skull cult of Mex-
ican art, with personal references through the character of the
church painter, with the Russian silent films (in the train of flagellants), with theatrical freemasonry, with God and the devil, with a
literary mixture of styles all the way from high-strung serenity to
badly camouflaged aphorisms—in truth a *Gesamtkunstwerk.*

Paris' arrow was poisoned and therefore he could kill Achilles by
shooting him in the tendon. But it is questionable whether one can
regard a work of art in such a physiological way. Unless the tendon
covers the whole body, unless the flaws radiate an all-pervading
poison, there may be good reason to examine what the film gives
us apart from the feeling of recognition, and to see if what is left—
the beauty of which no one seems to dispute—is in any vital way
threatened or deformed by the less appealing devices used by Bergman.

To begin with, let us establish that the beauty of the film is not
an aesthetic end in itself. The film deals with many things: for
instance, religious problems of faith, intolerance, religious madness;
it deals to a large extent with man's attitude towards death. All of
the themes enumerated here, and many more, belong to the so-
called fundamental questions. It is difficult to say anything new
about them. Therefore, if one considers it urgent to base a work of
art on such themes, a new form becomes obligatory. In Bergman the
new form is in this case identical with a unique pictorial and
dramatic beauty.

In the relationship of art to the fundamental questions there is
an alternative—in the indirect approach, in the symbolic realism
which is characteristic of de Sica's films. It is a more refined but
doubtless less dramatic alternative, and it demands in any case a
distance to personally urgent problems which Bergman as yet is
not capable of, except in the form of parodies and pastiches.

Hence the beauty of *The Seventh Seal* is functional and thereby
the merits of the film as a work of art have gained an inescapable
alibi.

But then what is it that Bergman is saying in such a beautiful and convincing way? What psychological truths or conflicts are conveyed by the different roles? The questions miss the point a little in that the roles are from the very beginning strongly typed. Most of them *are* nothing but represent something. The actor-as-clown, the good and innocent dreamer and his child-of-nature wife, the simple man of the people and his voluptuous woman, the skeptical squire accompanying the Crusader who struggles with his beliefs. In these parts there is as much truth as in the standard types of the commedia dell'arte—which means essentially that they are uninteresting as individuals and interesting only as symbols. It also explains the film's lack of thematic coherence. Within the frame of the dramatic action the actors are confronted with different situations, meant to give each role the occasion to react in precisely its characteristic way. Hence the seemingly rhapsodic nature of the film and the mutual independence of the sequences.

Bergman's intention with the film was probably not as strained as these views. For him the Crusader, the central figure in the film, is in all likelihood a reality more than a symbol. Those who have inclinations towards religious brooding no doubt see him differently from the way I do. Yet, what is of interest is that I, who am indifferent to the religious problems of the role, nevertheless am fascinated by its symbolic dimensions. Through dramatically tense close-ups of Max von Sydow's sculptural face, a Jacob's struggle is suggested, which, whether it is religious or not, cannot but fascinate and engage even a modern agnostic.

But what is unfortunate about these type roles is that they talk a great deal. Gunnel Lindblom has a great role in the film which she, with the exception of one cue of two words at the end of the film, plays altogether silently. Her mute performance is more than the finest acting achievement in the film. Her placement in the context, quite beyond the range of analytical method, is typical of Bergman's poetic feeling, his bold confidence. The squirrel in the sequence mentioned and Gunnel Lindblom are simply part of the film—the former as a playful dissolve, the latter as imaginatively enticing close-up.

In ordinary films the task of the dialogue is often to drag the action forward. But Bergman has literary ambitions and an indisputable literary talent. He has learnt to use his talent in comedies and there he is, like all jesters, invulnerable. But when he is serious in his self-preoccupied way, he exposes himself to great risks because of his unrestrained literary ambitions.

It is in fact surprising how often he succeeds in a film like *The Seventh Seal* in staying on the right side in his balancing between the sublime and the ludicrous. The sad thing is that the balancing itself is too noticeable—one follows the involute syntax and twisted superstructure of the dialogue with the same tension and expectation with which one follows a tightrope dancer (which in itself destroys the dramatic mood). One is prepared for an accident to occur and feels almost relieved when it only comes as one of the blunders that Harrie and Landquist are disturbed about.

A dialogue that oscillates between "May I offer you a drink" and "Follow that black car" can never be bad. Even in the most serious and ambitious film such a dialogue is necessary. A literary dialogue, in which the language sprouts in all its richness, has a function other than that of narrative. In literature and in the theater it shall suggest visions and moods that the film supplies with its own means.

Take the opening sequence of the film, the wild, desolate beach, the hawk [sea-eagle] still in the air, the silence, the slow, suggestively double-exposed, blinding supersolves, the horses at the shore, the knight and Death at the beautiful chess table—and then the solemn speech, like icing on a cake.

Take the pastoral scene with the wild strawberries, famous by now. An intense mood achieved by a simple lucidity, a natural beauty—and then the knight's cue that the memory of this meal, of this communion, which we in the cinema have just experienced with him, shall be "of a great adequacy" to him. Plop, said the frog.

Ingmar Bergman is a poet. He does not create in isolated images, as Sjöberg does, which would be too simple, but in a form of drama that is visually daring. Unfortunately he does not trust the power of his creative form of expression. Where nothing is lacking he adds the word, not the simple word but the literary word.

Harrie thought that the basis of the film, Bergman's own play *Wood Painting*, was much better as a play than *The Seventh Seal* is as a film. And yet it is in both cases largely a question of the same dialogue. But on the stage, where the word dominates, richness is the same as subtlety. In film, on the filled screen, the richness of the word becomes florid ornament.

The weaknesses in *The Seventh Seal*, in Bergman's oeuvre, can thus be explained. Somewhat regretfully, they can still be accepted by those who in their critical task have not been struck by puritanical fever. But what seems most essential in the film still remains: the portrait of the squire, the burning of the witch, the tavern sequence, and . . . the train of flagellants—a coherent modern theme beyond both *Wood Painting* and *The Saga of the Folkungs*.

Death, collective death in the form of the plague, is the *leitmotif* of the film. The Black Death gives us an inflamed picture of society, a collective presence of death that cannot be unreal to anyone who has heard of the H-bomb. The hysterical intolerance, the ruthless cruelty towards the individual, the merciless destructiveness and the drive for ecstatic self-annihilation are terribly relevant social realities. Through this collective walks the squire, a modern agnostic who himself is quite cruel, but not meaninglessly cruel; skeptical towards all and everything, not the least towards himself; but at the same time open to his fellow human beings, conscious of his own insufficiency, passive to a certain extent, but beyond that, energetic and responsible.

It is the first time such a person appears in Ingmar Bergman's work, at least in the kind of light he has chosen here. Earlier he appeared as a childish grimace, as an antireligious demon or a caricature but not as a person with a prototypal religious dignity. Here one discerns the contours of Camus' modern hero, a symbol of the integrity of man, of the individual. The portrait is not rich. Apparently Bergman has not yet dared give it the central role it deserves in modern drama. But the fate of the squire suggests at any rate modern man's dramatic relationship to his surroundings. Man's sluggish hopelessness is juxtaposed to man's courage and dignity, without a religious superstructure. This is more than social consciousness: it is the most urgent social message.

It is possible that this theme, which is new to Bergman, is the result of an unconscious and unintentional accident. If that is not the case, which one would like to hope, Bergman, the poet, has found something to create about which is worthy of his unique talent.

The Obligatory Scene in
THE SEVENTH SEAL
by ROBERT GESSNER

I. THE NATURE OF THE CINEMATIC OBLIGATORY SCENE

The moment when expectation is fulfilled is *la scène à faire*—
what William Archer, the English playwright and dramatic critic,
called the "obligatory scene." "It is precisely this expectation," wrote
the critic Francisque Sarcey, "mingled with uncertainty which is one
of the charms of the theater." There is a French expression: *Vous
allez avoir de quoi faire*—You have your work cut out. *Scène à faire*
is the scene to be made, almost inevitably toward the conclusion of
the drama.

How does this nineteenth-century dramatic observation apply to
twentieth-century cinema? Many contemporary films deliberately
ignore or unwittingly discard the obligatory scene, with varied
results. The question, regardless of fashion or style, centuries or
modes, deals with tensions and anticipations in storytelling. Film
audiences universally expect an acceleration of some sort, an ac-
cumulation of rising actions and reactions. The absence of an
anticipated fulfillment can be a frustration comparable to the interruption by commercials during televised movies. To be frustrated
in the viewing of any art is irritating, to say the least, and can be
nihilistic. What appears to be neglected in much of contemporary
cinema is an appreciation of the emotional need for anticipation.

More than audience psychology obliges the writer-director to go beyond excitement. He is obliged as a craftsman to fulfill the promises he planted in his opening scenes. If he is an artist, he is obliged to culminate the emotional experience he has been sharing with some sort of a significant catharsis—not necessarily through the "pity and fear" that Aristotle proposed.

"There are works of art that merely excite," wrote John Dewey in his *Art as Experience,* "in which activity is aroused without the composure of satisfaction, without fulfillment within the terms of the medium. Energy is left without organization. Dramas are then melodramatic; paintings of nudes are pornographic; the fiction that is read leaves us discontented with the world. . . ." The organization of energy—which for our purposes we might call "plot"—can be achieved, Dewey suggests, through symmetry and rhythm. "The connection of intensity and extensity and of both with tension is not a verbal matter," Dewey continues. "There is no rhythm save where there is alternation of compressions and releases."

The obligatory scene is a rhythm factor. Contemporary cinema has so much more compression of action and plastic imagery of movement than traditional drama that there exist both minor and major obligatory scenes. A screenplay may have half a dozen minor concentrations of intensity that are the goals of those sequences toward which the idea is moving. The major obligatory scene would be the goal of the entire action, the greatest compression and the most intense anticipation. What has been ordinarily called the "obligatory scene" is the obvious confrontation between warring characters, the long-awaited clash between hero and villain, "the big scene." David confronts Goliath and throws his stone; Hamlet at last kills the King; Golden Boy turns to brass.

After an obligatory scene the mind of the viewer should behave differently. No character leaves a cinematic obligatory scene the same as when he entered, or else it isn't obligatory. It is expository or narrative or flatly dramatic. . . .

. . . An overfulfillment [of the obligatory scene] is the case in *The Seventh Seal,* an allegorical encounter with death wherein a series of anticipations create a total of no less than six obligatory scenes. This pessimistic drama of man's quest for answers about God and death has exquisite moments of carefully chiseled photography— the vision, to name one, of the Virgin Mother strolling with the Christ Child through the meadow like princess and son. The concern of Bergman is how each of us faces death. The suspense is not in the when, but the how. With so many obligatory scenes Bergman appears to transcend the necessity for any of them (in surplus there is excess), and demonstrates that an audience can become involved without the traditional suspense of the obligatory scene, but purely on the sheer force of intelligence, style, performance, and theme. All the horrors of witch-burning, flagellations (*Totentanz*), rape, thievery, and deceit appear as sensational illustrations of an idea that is already explicit.

Here are the six obligatory scenes (translated by Lars Malmström and David Kushner). The first:

The KNIGHT *returns to the beach and falls on his knees. With his eyes closed and brow furrowed, he says his morning prayers. His hands are clenched together and his lips form the words silently. His face is sad and bitter. He opens his eyes and stares directly into the morning sun which wallows up from the misty sea like some bloated, dying fish. The sky is gray and immobile, a dome of lead. A cloud hangs mute and dark over the western horizon. High up, barely visible, a sea gull floats on motionless wings.[1] Its cry is weird and restless.*

The KNIGHT'S *large gray horse lifts its head and whinnies.* ANTONIUS BLOCK *turns around.*

Behind him stands a man in black. His face is very pale and he keeps his hands hidden in the wide folds of his cloak.

Knight: Who are you?

Death: I am Death.

Knight: Have you come for me?

Death: I have been walking by your side for a long time.

Knight: That I know.

Death: Are you prepared?

Knight: My body is frightened, but I am not.

Death: Well, there is no shame in that.

The KNIGHT *has risen to his feet. He shivers.* DEATH *opens his cloak to place it around the* KNIGHT'S *shoulders.*

Knight: Wait a moment.

Death: That's what they all say. I grant no reprieves.

Knight: You play chess, don't you?

A gleam of interest kindles in DEATH'S *eyes.*

[1] [Cf. note, p. 10.]

Knight Antonius Block makes a condition "that I may live as long as I hold out against you. If I win, you will release me."

Though the outcome is foreordained, curiosity centers upon the length of the reprieve. On this strung-out clothesline Bergman hangs his episodic sermons, propping their weight at regular intervals with poles. The second expected meeting occurs when the knight enters a confession booth—"The face of Death appears behind the grille for an instant, but the knight doesn't see him." The knight confesses his doubts over God—he is returning from a Crusade— "My life has been a futile pursuit, a wandering, a great deal of talk without meaning." He confides his tactic for beating the Devil at chess—"In the next move I'll shatter one of his flanks." Death replies: "I'll remember that."

DEATH *shows his face at the grille of the confession booth for a moment but disappears instantly.*

Knight: You've tricked and cheated me! But we'll meet again, and I'll find a way.

Death (invisible): We'll meet at the inn, and there we'll continue playing.

The third pole props up the story line before the inn scene:

The KNIGHT *picks up his chess game and carries it toward the beach. It is quiet and deserted; the sea is still.*

Death: I've been waiting for you.

Knight: Pardon me. I was detained for a few moments. Because I revealed my tactics to you, I'm in retreat. It's your move.

Death: Why do you look so satisfied?

Knight: Don't worry about my laughter; save your king instead.

Death: You're rather arrogant.

Knight: Our game amuses me.

Death: It's your move. Hurry up. I'm a little pressed for time.

Knight: I understand that you've a lot to do, but you can't get out of our game. It takes time.

The defiance of Death is a positive alteration that serves to heighten anticipation. The fourth meeting serves to postpone a decision, and, hence, to add further expectancy. The scene comes during the preparation for burning Tyan, the young girl accused of consorting with the devil:

They take her down from the cart and lead her toward the ladder and the stake. The KNIGHT *turns to the* MONK, *who remains seated in the cart.*

Knight: What have you done with the child?

Death (turns around and looks at him): Don't you ever stop asking questions?

Knight: No, I'll never stop.

Death appears next in the forest, but his encounter this time is with Skat, the lecherous actor, who has just feigned suicide to escape death at the hands of a cuckold smith, Plog. It is an amusing scene in which Bergman comments on actors' vanities: Skat is up a tree, which Death is sawing, and pleads—"my performance . . . my contract . . . Aren't there any special rules for actors?" The scene also reminds us that Death is more than a chessplayer. He can kill.

The sixth and final appearance of Death also occurs in the forest. It is curiously anticlimactical for an obligatory scene, since anticipation has run dry. Death takes the knight's queen. The knight does not move.

He pretends to be clumsy and knocks the chess pieces over with the hem of his coat. He looks up at DEATH.

Knight: I've forgotten how the pieces stood.

Death (laughs contentedly): But I have not forgotten. You can't get away that easily.

Death announces to Antonius Block that he is mated on the next move, and asks if the knight enjoyed his reprieve. Block admits he did:

Death: I'm happy to hear that. Now I'll be leaving you. When we meet again, you and your companions' time will be up.

Knight: And you will divulge your secrets.

Death: I have no secrets.

Knight: So you know nothing.

Death: I have nothing to tell.
The KNIGHT *wants to answer, but* DEATH *is already gone.*

The final image is a silhouette against a stormy sky of Death leading his troupe of dancers "toward the dark lands. . . ." The sight is witnessed by a symbolic Adam and Eve, the players Jof and wife Mia, who holds her son Mikael in her lap.

The Seventh Seal, we may note, suffers from a plethora of obligatory scenes, which are more like statements than dramatic resolutions.

COMMENTARIES

With *The Seventh Seal*
Ingmar Bergman Offers Us His Faust
ERIC ROHMER

◆◇◆

. . . The greatest merit of the film is to have been first of all a film—and one of the most beautiful films ever made—in spite of its abstract and theoretical subject matter. There is nothing in the film that makes it look like an illustration of a preconceived thesis. The author confides in us—and we have no trouble believing that his point of departure was not so much an idea as it was a picture. Themes dear to the painters and sculptors of the Middle Ages inspired him to the different motifs that he treats.

But this perfect understanding of medieval art would not in itself mean a sure success. It is not a question here of a more or less refined exercise in local color, such as one could see in Marcel Carné's *Visitors of the Evening* or in Alf Sjöberg's *The Road to Heaven*. If we had to find an equivalent we would have to turn back to the *Faust* of Murnau, a comparison we are invited to by the vast skies that open both works. . . .

André Bazin likes to show that in *The Passion of Joan of Arc*, the presence of a sole clump of real earth saves the film from artifice, from theatricality. Here [in *The Seventh Seal*] the equivalent of that clump of earth is found at each turn in the knight's itinerary: it is the foaming sea and the forest with its large, dark trees . . . which serve as a backrop for the quest of this modern Grail. It is even more the pearly light of the Nordic skies, unequalled by Bergman. When the knight discovers, in the halo of the sunset, that the imminence of death has doubled the price of the moment, we reach

"Avec Le septième sceau *Ingmar Bergman nous offre son Faust"* by *Eric Rohmer. From* Arts, *April 23–29, 1958. Reprinted by permission of the author. Translated from the French by Kristine Hughie and Birgitta Steene.*

one of the most intensely beautiful instants that cinematic art has ever offered us. . . .

There is certainly naivete in this allegory, but there is some naivete in every fable. It is the naivete proper to the great periods of art—here the Middle Ages, whose flavor Bergman has captured without any adulterating pedantry and thanks to his incomparable skill in transposing into cinematic terms the motifs that furnish him with the iconography on which he draws his inspiration. The figures and the forms he presents are never flat but seem the fruit of an original creation. His art is so frank, so new that we forget it for the problem it embodies. Rarely has the cinema been able to aim so high and realize so fully its ambitions.

The Seventh Seal
JOHN RUSSELL TAYLOR

◆◆

Technically the film is impeccable. The black-and-white photography of Gunnar Fischer is constantly striking (it is the sort of film which yields excellent stills, which may or may not be a good thing), with its crisp, clear deep-focus work, its very black blacks and very white whites. The story is told with admirable economy, no detail being wasted or missing its effect. The acting, when acting is called for (mainly from Max von Sydow and Gunnar Björnstrand), does perfectly everything required of it. And yet the film, despite all this and some genuinely enthralling moments, seems somehow too pale and remote, too patently composed as an illustration of its thesis. Its final effect, when all has been said in its favor, is rather lifeless, and lacking as it does the power of a completely

"The Seventh Seal" [editor's title] from Cinema Eye, Cinema Ear by John Russell Taylor (New York: Hill & Wang, 1964), p. 159. Reprinted by permission of Hill & Wang.

realized work of art to sweep aside objections, *The Seventh Seal* strikes one as making implicit claims for itself out of all proportion to its actual achievements. If a filmmaker sets out to make a cosmic drama of Life and Death, with a lot of Christian symbolism thrown in, he must expect to be judged by the most rigorous standards, and by such standards *The Seventh Seal* fails. It never finally convinces us, as it obviously intends to, that all its horrors, the rapes, tortures, flagellations, burnings, are valid expressions of a pessimistic world picture only lightly touched with hope; they remain, if not exactly sensational, at least rather pointless, overstating a case that should not need such determined emphasis.

Views and Reviews:
Bergman's *The Seventh Seal*
MICHAEL ROEMER

◆◇◆

In *The Seventh Seal* (1956), Bergman's personal preoccupations can no longer be ignored: they occupy center stage. A medieval knight, returned from the Crusades, seeks the meaning of life in a world racked by disease, superstition, and cruelty. He meets suffering and death at every turn, and his questions remain unanswered even as he himself joins the endless dance of death.

The rendering of reality is subjective. Antonius Block is no medieval knight but a modern man trying to find his way past doubt and despair. He moves through a series of allegorical encounters— with a group of traveling actors, a procession of flagellants, a young woman about to be burned as a witch, and with Death himself—as if in a dream. While the setting and some of the details are treated realistically, no attempt is made to give the story an objective real-

From "Bergman's Bag of Tricks" by Michael Roemer. From The Reporter *26, no. 4 (February 15, 1962): 38–39. Copyright 1962 by The Reporter Magazine Company. Reprinted by permission of the author and* The Reporter.

ity. The sequence of events is not logical but subjective: what happens does not happen *to* Block but *inside* him.

"A film for me," Bergman has said, "begins with something very vague—a chance remark or a bit of conversation, a hazy but agreeable event unrelated to any particular situation. . . . These are split-second impressions that disappear as quickly as they come, yet leave behind a mood—like pleasant dreams. It is a mental state, not an actual story, but one abounding in fertile associations and images. Most of all, it is a brightly colored thread sticking out of the dark sack of the unconscious. If I begin to wind up the thread, and do it carefully, a complete film will emerge."

Without wishing to question the often profound relationship between the origins of art and the unconscious, one wonders whether Bergman has left out an essential step: the substantiation or concretion of his material. By using images and feelings in the very form and sequence in which they evidently emerge out of his unconscious, he is building a highly subjective structure that runs the danger of being shapeless and unstable. In a medium that communicates through concrete situations and physical realities, he is depending on abstractions and a highly personal imagery.

The Seventh Seal, in spite of its visual preoccupation with gouging, branding, and burning, has a curiously abstract quality. The dialogue is literary. Shortly before the end the knight—aware that he must die—shares a meal with the young actor. "I shall always remember this moment," he says. "The silence, the twilight, the bowls of strawberries and milk, your faces in the evening light. Mikael sleeping, Jof with his lyre. I'll try to remember what we have talked about. I'll carry the memory between my hands as carefully as if it were a bowl filled to the brim with fresh milk. And it will be an adequate sign—it will be enough for me." Without this lengthy explanation, one would have no insight into the feelings of Antonius Block; the situation itself does not render them. In Kurosawa's *Living* a man who is dying of cancer stops on his way home from work to look at the evening sky. "It's beautiful," he says to his companion, "but I have no time." No further explanation is needed, for the man and his feelings are clear.

In *The Seventh Seal* what happens on the screen, moment after moment, is essentially a series of conventions: conventions of action, dialogue, imagery. Most moviemakers, by setting up a sequence of incidents and images that have a proven effect, play on the feelings of their audience—very much as a writer of detective fiction plays on their curiosity. The feelings are not rendered; they are simply cited; they do not find their own vocabulary but use the secondhand language that most films share, a language that is changed only when the audience no longer responds.

If at first glance the action and imagery of *The Seventh Seal* seem original, it is largely because Bergman is working with conventions that are unfamiliar in motion pictures and because he uses them with obvious conviction. Horses against the sea, the black-robed figure of Death, stormy skies, dark forests, chiaroscuro landscapes, towns emptied by plague—an entire arsenal of nineteenth-century romantic imagery is mustered with great skill and feeling. We are susceptible to these images because the screen gives them an appearance of dimension and reality they have long lost in painting and literature. We are susceptible, furthermore, because Bergman uses them to conjure up the great themes of life and art: suffering, joy, death, love, youth, faith, good and evil. But just as the images are essentially hollow and derivative, so the vast metaphysical scope of the film is nothing more than a sincere but thin evocation of great themes. The thematic material, Block's questions about the meaning of life, are—like the imagery—used as a kind of incantation: lulling and effective until one begins to examine them. While the intention is undoubtedly serious and the effect often hypnotic, the film is vague and takes place in limbo. . . .

The Seventh Seal
LINDSAY ANDERSON

◆◇◆

Ingmar Bergman's *The Seventh Seal* is an extraordinary Gothic creation, a fifteenth-century fable which has all the surprise and

The Seventh Seal *by Lindsay Anderson. From Edinburgh Film Festival Catalogue, 1957. Reprinted by permission of Lindsay Anderson.*

suggestiveness of legend, and a quite marvelous feeling of period-medieval lyricism and cruelty, sense of dread and sense of wonder all commingled. Returning from a Crusade, a knight meets Death on the seashore. But he doubts: he is not ready to die: he challenges Death to a game of chess. He cannot win, but he holds his enemy off for a time as he journeys on towards home with his skeptical stoical servant. They fall in with other travelers: there is a plague, a girl is burned as a witch, they are joined by a strolling player (who sees visions) and his wife and child. These innocents escape; but the rest of the company must obey their destiny, and Death takes them off up the skyline in the end, a macabre, silhouetted line of dancers. The symbolism is rich and powerful, but the film never loses its quality of story—a Gothic tale (I was reminded of Baroness Blixen). The style, too, has the right, uncompromising simplicity: it is highly sophisticated, of course, but never bizarre. Bergman is really somebody.

"Y" Certificate

NINA HIGGIN

◆◇◆

Showing at Cinephone this week is a double-feature programme, *Street of Shame* and *Isle of Levant*. Both films are of unusual crudeness and vulgarity. Their impact is negligible, and I don't propose to give them the distinction of a review.

Far more shocking are the intellectual obscenities of the Swedish film *The Seventh Seal*. . . .

It is an allegorical film, with high-flown pretensions about a knight of the Crusades who returns disillusioned, to see, through his diseased mind, a plague-ridden world of human depravity.

"'Y' Certificate" by Nina Higgin. From The Daily Worker, *March 8, 1958. Reprinted by permission of the publisher.*

He lifts no helping hand, for to him, life and death are equally futile.

It has been made by that master of cinema technique Ingmar Bergman, and its excruciating sadism has earned it an X certificate.

I give it a Y certificate—my own invention, designed to exclude everybody!

The Movie-Makers
PENELOPE HOUSTON

◆◇◆

. . . Bergman has behind him a volume of work which few people of his generation in the cinema can begin to equal. In a country with only a limited output of films at the best of times, and where strike action has more than once brought the industry almost to a dead stop, he has directed or collaborated on more than twenty-five films. He has written many of his own scripts; he has assembled that dazzling company of players—Max von Sydow, Gunnar Björnstrand, Eva Dahlbeck, Harriet Andersson—whose performances he orchestrates through film after film. More has been written about him, in wilder and more extreme terms, than about any other postwar filmmaker: his symbolism has been detailed and catalogued; his childhood, in a strict Swedish parsonage, examined; his work has been analyzed in terms of Sweden's notorious "neutrality complex"; he has been called a masochist, a misogynist, a puritan, and, in a cruelly enlightening phrase, "the best German director of the postwar cinema." Five years or so ago, when it was impossible to pick up a magazine without finding the obligatory Bergman article, phrases like "the Shakespeare of the cinema" were tossed freely around.

"The Movie-Makers" by Penelope Houston. From The Contemporary Cinema. *(Baltimore: Penguin Books, 1963), pp. 163–65. Copyright © 1963 by Penelope Houston. Reprinted by permission of the publisher.*

To attract all this, a filmmaker needs to have something oracular in his make-up, in the sense that one consults the oracle not for a clear message, but for the satisfaction of deciphering the riddle. Although Bergman's symbolism is far from impenetrable, his attitude to his characters, stretched so agonizingly on the rack of his imagination, invites speculation. Those middle-aged married couples, quarrelling so bitterly in cars and trains; the old professor in *Wild Strawberries*, his life a blank filled in by the symbols of academic achievement, taking a pilgrimage through his past; the charlatan in *The Face*, a magician in spite of himself; the father in *The Virgin Spring*, conducting a ritual purification before embarking on the slaughter of the men who have raped and killed his daughter; the knight at his chess game with Death in *The Seventh Seal*: they all dance to the strings pulled by their creator, expressions of his ironic despair at the Russian roulette of existence, his questioning of the nature of belief. Bergman can appear almost sadistically brutal to these people of his invention; and then, suddenly, he lets up, flooding the screen with images of innocence and delight. Pain and pleasure alternate: the revolver hammer clicks again on an empty chamber, and the relief is exquisite. These flashes of happiness and tranquillity—the picnic in *The Seventh Seal*, the shots of lovers by lakesides, of sunlight and water, the rapturous surge of ironic glee at the end of *The Face*—are outdoor moments, summer moments held against the long Swedish night.

Bergman has worked through a Germanic brand of expressionism, straight realism (notably in early films such as *Hamnstad*), the historical morality of *The Seventh Seal*; he has juggled with dreams and reality, past and present, truth and illusion, the line that separates the artist as a performer from the artist as a man; he has told us that it is both necessary and miserable to love; he has taken us on a tour of the Swedish soul, so that no article purporting to explain that enigmatic country is now complete without its set of Bergman references; he has worked around the themes of destiny and free will. To his brilliance as a *metteur en scène,* a manipulator of effect, the crystalline tragicomedy of *Smiles of a Summer Night* offers sufficient witness. He has made films which everyone admires, and films which only the extreme Bergman enthusiasts want to see again; he has done so much that commentators on his work can pick up half a dozen separate threads as guides through the Bergman maze. Yet the mists thicken round the oracle, whose northern cave provides such a bleak frontage on life. If one finds his world antipathetic, it may be because, as in a Graham Greene novel, one feels that in shutting off the doors of escape to his characters the artist is taking over the role of destiny. Bergman robs a mother of her child, sends a witch to the burning, puts the revolver with its single bullet to the temple of a man weary of life. Is it fate, or Bergman, who decides who dies and who lives? It is this sense of the ringmaster, touching up an act with a flick of his whip, that sets up a resistance.

Plot Synopsis

Weary and disillusioned, **Antonius Block** and his squire Jöns have returned from a ten-year stay in the Holy Land. Upon their arrival in Sweden they learn that the country is ravaged by the bubonic plague. Death, dressed in black cape and with a chalky white face, has in fact come to claim Antonius Block. But the knight challenges Death to a game of chess and thus gets a respite, which forms the main action of the film.

Traveling through fourteenth-century Sweden, Antonius Block and Jöns meet a number of people who all experience a great sense of imminence, for they know that they may soon die. Among them are a smith and his unfaithful wife, Lisa; Raval, a sadistic priest and now a thief; a mute girl who becomes Jöns' housekeeper and companion; a church painter whose task it is to paint realistic pictures of the dance of death; a witch, Tyan, who is burnt at the stake believing that she is communicating with the devil; and a troupe of actors, including the juggler Jof and his wife Mia, whose performance is at one time interrupted by a train of flagellants.

From time to time Death intercepts the knight on his travel. Posing as a confessor in the church where the knight has gone to pray, Death learns of the knight's scheme in the chess game. Before Antonius Block is checkmated, however, he has distracted Death so that Jof and Mia are able to escape the plague with their infant son Mikael. The knight, on the other hand, returns to his castle with his company, only to wait for Death who comes to claim him, his wife and his entourage. The film ends as Death leads his victims in a dance across the hills into the dark lands. They are seen silhouetted against the evening sky by Jof, the visionary artist, who describes to Mia what he sees.

Outline

I. INTRODUCTION

Oratorio music against dramatic clouds.
Abrupt silence. A sea-eagle glides against the sky.
A voice begins to read from the Apocalypse.
Cliffs. Overhead shot of horses on the beach.

Medium shots of Knight next to chess set, of Squire asleep, of horses.
Close-up of Knight.
Shot of ocean.
Close-up of Squire.

II. ON THE BEACH

Camera moves in on Knight, contemplating.
Knight goes down to sea to wash himself, then tries to pray.
Close-up of Knight.
Close-up of a chess set against cliffs and ocean.
Dissolve.

Death appears.
Knight rummages in bag, then notices Death.
Close-up of chalky white face of Death.
As Death walks up towards Knight, his cape covers the screen for a moment.
During ensuing dialogue, camera moves back and forth between Knight and Death.
Knight asks for a delay, proposing a game of chess. Death accepts. He draws black.
Dissolve of Knight and Death playing chess.

III. On the Coast

Knight steps over Squire who wakes up. Dissolve.
Overhead view of beach. Dissolve.

The Squire riding, singing a bawdy song.
Series of medium shots of Knight and Squire riding.

IV. On the Plateau

Knight and Squire pass a shepherd seated on the ground.
Squire goes up to him. Shot of shepherd from behind.
Squire turns head of man.
Shock close-up of face of cadaver.

The Knight and Squire continue riding. Dissolve.

V. Jof and His Wagon

The camera comes to rest on Jof's wagon.
Close-up of Jof, Mia, and Skat, sleeping.
Jof wakes up, chases a mosquito, goes outside, talks to his
horse and starts juggling.
Celestial music. Jof has vision of the Virgin Mary, walking a
naked child.
Jof rubs his eyes, runs into wagon to tell Mia of his vision.
Mia skeptical.
Skat wakes up, complaining.
Jof, Mia, and child go outside.
Shot of baby.
Close-up of Mia going to sleep on Jof's shoulder as he sings
to her.
Skat comes out with death mask, complaining about the role
he has to play.
Skat hangs death mask on a tree branch and goes back into
wagon.

Close-up of mask.
Mia watches Jof juggle. Dissolve.

VI. Squire and Painter in the Church

Knight and Squire arrive at church and enter it.
Squire meets a painter who is working on a fresco.
Panning of painting.
Close-up of victim of the plague while painter describes symptoms of disease.
Shot of flagellants painted on the wall. Dissolve.

VII. In the Church: The Knight's Prayer

Fade-in on Knight at altar.
Close-up of face of suffering Christ.
Shot of priest in confession booth.
Knight speaks: "I want knowledge, not suppositions. . . ."
Close-up of Christ's face.
Knight turns to priest, expresses his doubts; reveals his strategy in the chess game.
Close-up of Death, turned away from Knight, and of Knight outside the bars of the confession booth.
Death reveals himself to Knight, then leaves.

Knight raises his hand and looks at it, lifts it to his temple.
Soft background music as Knight speaks: "This is my hand. I can move it, feel the blood pulsing through it. The sun is still high in the sky and I, Antonius Block, am playing chess with Death."

VIII. Return to Squire and Painter

Both are slightly drunk. Squire paints a caricature of himself, jokes about the Knight's Crusade to the Holy Land.

The Knight passes by, picks up caricature, leaves.
Squire follows him.

IX. Outside the Church: The Witch

A young girl in the stocks.
Close-up of monk mumbling from a book.

Soldier appears with bowl of bloody paste, used to chase away the devil.
Squire holds his nose.

Knight looks at girl and asks her: "Have you seen the devil?"
Monk tells him to stay away.
Whining, then terrible moaning of girl as Knight and Squire leave.

X. KNIGHT AND SQUIRE ON HORSEBACK

Squire rides along singing. Knight stops him.
Fade-in on cluster of farmhouses.
Squire walks up to abandoned farm, enters, discovers dead woman on the floor.
Hides as he hears steps.
Raval, the expriest, climbs down from loft; steals bracelet of dead woman.
Close-up of Mute Girl who has entered.

XI. AT THE FARM

Raval threatens Girl.
Squire appears behind door.
Close-up of Squire attacking Raval. Girl screams and he stops.
Dissolve as Squire and Girl leave.

XII. OUTSIDE THE FARM HOUSE

Squire tries to kiss Mute Girl at the well.
Asks her to follow him. Leaves.
Girl hesitates but runs after him.

XIII. ON THE STAGE OUTSIDE THE INN

Fade-in on stage where Jof, Mia, and Skat are performing.
Series of close-ups of Mia, Jof (as cuckolded husband), Skat (dressed up as a cock), Lisa, and Plog, the smith.

Skat hit by object from the crowd. Exits.
Jof and Mia sing song about "the Hen and the Cock."

XIV. SKAT AND LISA

Skat sees Lisa. He goes to meet her, walking like a prancing cock. Jof's and Mia's song is heard.
As Skat and Lisa disappear, chicken runs out of bushes.

XV. PROCESSION OF FLAGELLANTS

Jof's and Mia's song is drowned by the singing of Dies Irae.
Train of flagellants, carrying huge crosses and lashing each other.
Close-up of Knight, Squire and Mute Girl.
Panning of crowd.
Close-up of a young girl. Then crowd scene.
Close-ups of Christ figure on crucifix, of children in crowd, of young girl.
Shot of flagellants kneeling. Hysterical praying.
Monk begins to preach next to crucifix; Mia and Jof in background.
Series of close-ups of Knight, Monk, old men, girl crying, a skull.
Flagellants pick up crucifix and leave. Singing.
Overhead shot of train of flagellants. Dissolve.
Shot of ground, empty.

XVI. AT THE OPEN PLACE

Squire, Knight, and Mute Girl seated outside inn.
Plog, the smith, arrives looking for his wife.
Squire tells him to go to the inn.

XVII. AT THE INN

Customers at the Inn discuss the effect of the plague upon people.
There is talk of Judgment Day.

Close-ups of merchants and hostess.
General sound of voices and clinking of glasses.

Raval tries to sell bracelet to Jof, who refuses it.
Plog wants to kill Jof because he is an actor.
Raval forces Jof to stand on his head and to dance a bear dance at knife point.
Series of shots of customers laughing and of Jof's legs, moving frantically.
Close-up of Jof's face. Customers beat rhythm with their goblets.
Jof falls.
Squire enters. Silence. Close-up of Raval's face.
Squire marks Raval's face with knife.
Jof flees, picking up bracelet.
Close-up of Raval, wounded.

XVIII. In Front of the Wagon

Fade-in on Knight, playing chess by himself.
Knight sees Mia and talks to her about Mikael.
Jof arrives. Happy family scene.
Knight is introduced and invited to a repast of strawberries and fresh milk. Singing of birds.
Squire and Mute Girl arrive. Close-up of Mia.
Knight talks about his marriage. Taking the bowl of milk he speaks: "I shall always remember this moment . . ."
Background music of Jof with lyre.
Knight returns to chess set.
Death comes into frame.
Close-up of chess set.
Medium shot of Knight and Death playing, with wagon in background.
Death asks Knight about Jof and Mia. Dramatic music.

XIX. In Front of the Inn

Fade-in on Inn.
Plog and Squire talking about love.
Close-up of Plog, crying.

Exit of Plog and Squire. Outside, Plog tries to embrace Jof.
Company leaves. Fade-out.

XX. IN THE FOREST

Wagon traveling through forest.
Meeting of Plog and Lisa, who is accompanied by Skat.
Close-ups of Plog and Skat insulting each other.
Plog assisted by Squire. Medium shot, dominated by Squire.

Skat acts out his suicide.

XXI. SKAT IN THE TREE

Skat recovers from his fake suicide. Climbs a tree.
Death appears.
Close-up of Skat, singing to himself.
Sound of sawing.
Overhead shot of Death sawing off tree.
Series of shots of Death and Skat, exchanging cues.
Tree falling.
Close-up of stump. Squirrel runs up picking at the bark.

XXII. IN THE FOREST

Eery mood of forest at night. Dramatic music. Dissolve.
Branches against dark sky. Dissolve.
Series of close-ups of company.

Cart with Witch arrives. Squeaking sounds. Shouts of
soldiers.
Squire helps soldiers push cart through mud.
Medium shot of Witch chained in iron.
The cart drives on. Somber music. Dissolve.

XXIII. AT THE STAKES

Knight and company arrive. Stakes, skulls on ground.

Squire needles the soldiers. Sound of hammer and nails.

Medium shot of Knight and Witch.
Close-up of Knight outside bars of wagon.
Close-up of Witch: "Look into my eyes."
Close-up of Knight: "I see nothing."

Knight and Death (dressed as monk): "Don't you ever stop asking?"

Close-up of Witch, raised on ladder.

Squire and Knight, flames in background.
Close-up of Knight giving drug to Witch; holds her head.
Burning fire, soldiers.
Series of close-ups of Mute Girl, Squire and Knight, Witch on ladder, Jof and Mia. Dramatic music.
Wagon leaves. Witch dies. Dissolve.

XXIV. NIGHT IN THE FOREST

Fade-in on forest at night.
Overhead shot of Jof lighting a torch.
Close-up of Knight and chess set.
Close-up of Mia and Jof.
Medium shots of Lisa (crying), Plog, Squire, and of Knight.

Raval arrives, stricken by the plague. Screaming, gurgling sound, convulsive sobs.
Squire prevents Mute Girl from giving water to Raval.
Raval dies, his scream cut off in the middle.

Jof sees Death playing chess with Knight.
Jof flees with Mia and Michael. Dramatic music.

Knight pretends to be clumsy and knocks over chess pieces.
Jof's wagon disappears.
Death rearranges pieces and tells Knight he will be mated in the next move.
Close-up of Death with staring eyes. Dissolve.

XXV. Jof and Mia in the Wagon

Jof and Mia fleeing through forest. Loud singing. Sound of strong wind. Flickering light.

They stop and huddle inside wagon. Jof says it is the Angel of Death passing by.
Wagon canvas flutters and beats in the wind. Rain and thunder.
Dissolve.

XXVI. The Knight's Castle

Knight and company arrive at castle. Thunder and lightning.
Wife greets them.
Close-ups of Wife and Knight talking. Dissolve on Knight.

Fade-in on face of Mute Girl.
Shot of all, seated at the table. Wife reads from book of Apocalypse. Three knocks are heard.

Knight sends Squire to open the gate. He finds no one. Silence.
Close-up of face of Mute Girl.

All get up and look towards entrance. Music. Tears down face of Mute Girl. Silence.

Mute Girl advances towards Death who has entered.
Wife wishes him welcome.
Plog presents Lisa.
Knight cries to heaven.
Squire: "No one hears your complaint."

Mute Girl kneels, speaks for the first time: "It is finished!"
Dissolve.

XXVII. AT JOF'S AND MIA'S WAGON

>Wagon against quiet sea. Clear sky.
>Close-up of Jof seeing Dance of Death. Dissolve.
>
>Dance of Death silhouetted against sky. Dissolve.
>
>Close-ups of Jof and of Mia and child.
>Departure of wagon. Lyre music and singing.

Script Extract

The knight is kneeling before a small altar. It is dark and quiet around him. The air is cool and musty. Pictures of saints look down on him with stony eyes. Christ's face is turned upward, His mouth open as if in a cry of anguish. On the ceiling beam there is a representation of a hideous devil spying on a miserable human being. The knight hears a sound from the confession booth and approaches it. The face of Death appears behind the grille for an instant, but the knight doesn't see him.

Knight: I want to talk to you as openly as I can, but my heart is empty.

Death doesn't answer.

Knight: The emptiness is a mirror turned toward my own face. I see myself in it, and I am filled with fear and disgust.

Death doesn't answer.

Knight: Through my indifference to my fellow men, I have isolated myself from their company. Now I live in a world of phantoms. I am imprisoned in my dreams and fantasies.
Death: And yet you don't want to die.
Knight: Yes, I do.
Death: What are you waiting for?
Knight: I want knowledge.

From Four Screenplays of Ingmar Bergman *translated by David Kushner and Lars Malmström (New York: Simon & Schuster, Inc., 1960), pp. 111–13, 136–38. Copyright © 1960 by Simon & Schuster, Inc. Also published separately in 1968 by Lorrimer Publishing, London. Reprinted by permission of Simon & Schuster, Inc., and Lorrimer Publishing. This translation differs slightly from the English subtitles used in the film when it was released in the United States.*

Death: You want guarantees?

Knight: Call it whatever you like. Is it so cruelly inconceivable to grasp God with the senses? Why should he hide himself in a mist of half-spoken promises and unseen miracles?

Death doesn't answer.

Knight: How can we have faith in those who believe when we can't have faith in ourselves? What is going to happen to those of us who want to believe but aren't able to? And what is to become of those who neither want to nor are capable of believing?

The knight stops and waits for a reply, but no one speaks or answers him. There is complete silence.

Knight: Why can't I kill God within me? Why does He live on in this painful and humiliating way even though I curse Him and want to tear Him out of my heart? Why, in spite of everything, is He a baffling reality that I can't shake off? Do you hear me?

Death: Yes, I hear you.

Knight: I want knowledge, not faith, not suppositions, but knowledge. I want God to stretch out His hand toward me, reveal Himself and speak to me.

Death: But He remains silent.

Knight: I call out to Him in the dark but no one seems to be there.

Death: Perhaps no one is there.

Knight: Then life is an outrageous horror. No one can live in the face of death, knowing that all is nothingness.

Death: Most people never reflect about either death or the futility of life.

Knight: But one day they will have to stand at that last moment of life and look toward the darkness.

Death: When *that* day comes . . .

Knight: In our fear, we make an image, and that image we call God.

Death: You are worrying . . .

Knight: Death visited me this morning. We are playing chess together. This reprieve gives me the chance to arrange an urgent matter.

Death: What matter is that?

Knight: My life has been a futile pursuit, a wandering, a great deal of talk without meaning. I feel no bitterness or self-reproach because the lives of most people are very much like this. But I will use my reprieve for one single meaningful deed.

Death: Is that why you are playing chess with Death?

Knight: He is a clever opponent, but up to now I haven't lost a single man.

Death: How will you outwit Death in your game?

Knight: I use a combination of the bishop and the knight which he hasn't yet discovered. In the next move I'll shatter one of his flanks.

Death: I'll remember that.

Death shows his face at the grille of the confession booth for a moment but disappears instantly.

Knight: You've tricked and cheated me! But we'll meet again, and I'll find a way.

Death (invisible): We'll meet at the inn, and there we'll continue playing.

The knight raises his hand and looks at it in the sunlight which comes through the tiny window.

Knight: This is my hand. I can move it, feel the blood pulsing through it. The sun is still high in the sky and I, Antonius Block, am playing chess with Death.

He makes a fist of his hand and lifts it to his temple.

*   *   *

Jöns comes walking slowly down the hill, closely followed by the girl. Mia points with her spoon.

Mia: Do you want some strawberries?

Jof: This man saved my life. Sit down, my friend, and let us be together.

Mia (stretches herself): Oh, how nice this is.

Knight: For a short while.

Mia: Nearly always. One day is like another. There is nothing strange about that. The summer, of course, is better than the winter, because in summer you don't have to be cold. But spring is best of all.

Jof: I have written a poem about the spring. Perhaps you'd like to hear it. I'll run and get my lyre. (*He sprints toward the wagon.*)

Mia: Not now, Jof. Our guests may not be amused by your songs.

Jöns (politely): By all means. I write little songs myself. For example, I know a very funny song about a wanton fish which I doubt that you've heard yet.

The knight looks at him.

Jöns: You'll not get to hear it either. There are persons here who don't appreciate my art and I don't want to upset anyone. I'm a sensitive soul.

Jof has come out with his lyre, sits on a small, gaudy box and plucks at the instrument, humming quietly, searching for his melody. Jöns yawns and lies down.

Knight: People are troubled by so much.

Mia: It's always better when one is two. Have you no one of your own?

Knight: Yes, I think I had someone.

Mia: And what is she doing now?

Knight: I don't know.

Mia: You look so solemn. Was she your beloved?

Knight: We were newly married and we played together. We laughed a great deal. I wrote songs to her eyes, to her nose, to her beautiful little ears. We went hunting together and at night we danced. The house was full of life . . .

Mia: Do you want some more strawberries?

Knight (shakes his head): Faith is a torment, did you know that? It is like loving someone who is out there in the darkness but never appears, no matter how loudly you call.

Mia: I don't understand what you mean.

Knight: Everything I've said seems meaningless and unreal while I sit here with you and your husband. How unimportant it all becomes suddenly.

He takes the bowl of milk in his hand and drinks deeply from it several times. Then he carefully puts it down and looks up, smiling.

Mia: Now you don't look so solemn.

Knight: I shall remember this moment. The silence, the twilight, the bowls of strawberries and milk, your faces in the evening light. Mikael sleeping, Jof with his lyre. I'll try to remember what we have talked about. I'll carry this memory between my hands as carefully as if it were a bowl filled to the brim with fresh milk. (*He turns his face away and looks out toward the sea and the colorless gray sky.*) And it will be an adequate sign—it will be enough for me.

He rises, nods to the others and walks down toward the forest. Jof continues to play on his lyre. Mia stretches out on the grass.

The knight picks up his chess game and carries it toward the beach. It is quiet and deserted; the sea is still.

WOOD PAINTING
A Morality Play
by INGMAR BERGMAN

CHARACTERS

The Narrator	The Smith
The Girl	Maria
John	The Actor
The Knight	Lisa
The Witch	Karin
Time: fourteenth century.	Place: Sweden.

Narrator: The scene of our play was suggested by a mural that adorns the right wall of the vestibule of a little church in southern Småland. The painting dates from the end of the fourteenth century and its subject is the deadly plague that ravaged this province and many others in the neighborhood. The artist is unknown. But I've called the play *Wood Painting* and adhere more or less to the action shown in the mural, which begins at the small windows of the entryway, where the sun is playing over the quiet green landscape, and ends twelve feet away in a dark corner where the final incidents occur in the grayish, rain-laden dawn . . .

The Girl: Stop! You mustn't go further!

John: I guess you don't know who we are . . . I don't blame you!

The Girl: I'm sorry, but you can't cross the border.

John: Why doesn't your father, your husband, or your brother come out and try to stop us?

The Girl: My father hasn't come back from the war. My husband died three days ago. And my brother is sick.

John: I think I'll go in and have a little talk with your brother. He'll know me . . . and my master, too.

The Girl: Don't do it!

John: I can see why you're scared. We're so ugly . . . in these filthy rags and tatters . . . our horses gone . . . All the same, we're no criminals . . .

The Girl: But we have the plague.

John: Oh, my! That's awful . . . disgusting . . . terrible . . . My, oh my!

The Girl: And there's no remedy. No place of refuge. No one can escape. Don't you smell fire? It's been lying over the forest since early this morning.

John: Well, now that you mention it, I do smell smoke.

The Girl: They burned a witch at the crossroads this morning. They said she was to blame for the plague. She even confessed that she slept with the Black Fiend . . . so they burned her.

John: Well, then everything is all right. You've got to keep a close watch over those damned witches, because if they're not scaring up a plague, they're up to some other deviltry.

The Knight (from a distance): Come on, John. Don't stand there talking such nonsense!

The Girl: What is your master's name?

John: His name is Antonius Block, and he's your master as well as mine. For ten years we squatted in the Holy Land where snakes bit us, bugs stung us, wild animals attacked us, pagans slaughtered us, the wine poisoned us, the women loused us up, the lice devoured us, and fevers melted us down—all for the greater glory of God.

The Knight (from a distance): Do I have to beat you before you quit your babbling?

John: Why are you throwing sticks at me, Milord? I know whereof I speak. That Crusade of ours was so stupid that only a real idealist could have dreamed it up. Well, so long, my girl, the knight and I don't own a thing between us, so we can't reward you for your information. You'll have to render your bill when we meet each other in heaven—that is, if you ever get there.

The KNIGHT *and* JOHN *walk off in silence. Faint music.*

The Girl: They ought to take my advice, turn back, and go through the healthy countries. They haven't seen the hands or the eyes of the people dying of the plague . . . the blood foaming from their noses and mouths. They haven't seen the boils on their necks, larger each morning than they were the night before, and oozing pus. Big as a baby's head sometimes, while the bodies wither and shrink around the swelling until the limbs are like ropes and the people go mad. They spring out of their beds in agony, bite their hands, tear open their arteries with their fingernails, and their screams make the clouds burst. They dance in their beds, over the floors, at their fireplaces, in the meadows . . . then they fall, pant for breath, and die in the barns, in the yards, in the ditches, and on the banks of the river. People run away from the sick villages, far away to the north, but all the time a shadow follows them, a very Grave Gentleman.

Silence. Footsteps cease.

John: Poor little John . . . the sun has hardly set and the forest is so dark . . . There's a big crab sitting between my ribs . . . squeezing my heart. Suppose I try to sing a little song—
Sings.

> In the sea the fishes play
> And stately ships go on their way
> While here on land men die like flies—

Suddenly breaks off.

Are you afraid, little John? I say, are you afraid, little John? No! Not the tiniest bit afraid, little John? Yes!! I'm so scared that right this minute I'd be having an awful accident if my stomach weren't as empty as eternity.
Pause.

Who are you, my beautiful girl? Aren't you afraid of the dark?
The Witch: May I join you?

John: My master and I were just thinking of taking a rest. We're a bit tired. You see, we've just come back from a little stroll . . . from the Holy Land.

The Witch: Then I'll rest, too.

John: Good. Let's go into those bushes over there.

The Witch: What for?

John: We could do a little berry-picking. It's been such a long time.

The Witch: If you knew whom you were talking to, you wouldn't ask me to pick berries, or anything else, for that matter.

John: Well, who are you, if I may ask?

The Witch: I'm the witch they burned at the crossroads this morning.

John: Then you shouldn't be sitting here, if you're dead.

The Witch: I certainly am dead.

John: Then you are a ghost, and I don't believe in ghosts . . . so you don't exist, and you can't go on sitting here, annoying me and my master . . . unless we're dead, too, and have turned into ghosts. If that's the case, I don't know how it happened, but I won't give a damn about anything and won't say another word until Judgment Day.

The Witch: Did you and your master take part in the execution, by any chance?

John: No, unfortunately we didn't. We just happened to be out of town.

The Witch: Towards morning, I fell asleep for a while but I woke up almost at once. People were shouting outside the jail. I was afraid and I cried but it was useless, because everything was settled. I climbed up to the little window in the wall and looked down into the yard. I saw the cart they were going to take me away in . . . the priest was there, too . . . but I couldn't see the hangman. The sun was rising. There wasn't a single cloud in the sky. It looked hollow. I stood there staring at the people and I began to see their faces more clearly; and their chattering voices sounded like evil bird-calls . . . Suddenly I looked at my hands, that were clawing at the stone wall, and I saw that my nails were broken and black with blood and my knuckles were white, but my strength had not left me. Then I heard voices in the passage and the door was flung open. I fell down from the wall and lay with my head on the rough planks of the floor that stank of rotten straw. They bent down and grabbed me by the waist, pulled my shoulders back, and locked an iron collar around my neck. It was cold, and I shivered. I shivered so I couldn't speak, couldn't cry, couldn't walk. But they pulled my "necklace" so that I had to go along. They dragged me down the stone steps and through a long passageway, and each time I fell I thought I'd be choked to death. They always pulled me up by the collar. They didn't touch my body as the other watchmen did. They didn't laugh and joke with me like those who cut off my hair. They were quiet and scared. They just kept pulling at the collar because they were scared. They knew that He was following me, clutching my skirt.

Then they opened the doors, and the sun struck me in the face, and it was like a cry in the sun, and the morning breeze raised the dust and flung it into our faces.

Pause.

I was sitting in the cart, riding backwards, bound down so that my head rested on my breast . . . and when the cart jogged along the road, it hurt, because the iron cut into my flesh, but I didn't cry. The pain helped me, the stones in the road helped me, the squeaking of the wheels helped me. I closed my eyes and the sun burned in red waves through my lids. I heard the treading of hundreds of feet and the dust from the road was like smoke. I felt the people around me panting, I felt the pounding of their pulses, I felt their wide staring eyes—but no one uttered a sound.

Pause.

When we came to the place at the crossroads, they loosened my chains and I lifted my face to the sky. Above the fir trees, above the world, there were thin streaks of clouds, like fingers. Then I smelt the smoke of the fire; it poured down from the great heap of logs they had raised, and everyone began to cough. The fire flared up in a big fanlike flame and our faces burned from the heat. Then I turned around and saw Him standing behind me . . . and He smiled faintly, and His eyes became round and clear, and He came quite close to me . . . I felt His breath against my cheek . . . and He put His hand on my hip . . .

Pause.

Then I turned toward the stake and could barely make out the faces of all the people behind it. I raised my hands above my head and spread my fingers; I rose on my toes and stretched myself as far as I could. Then I laughed and laughed, but it sounded like a little child's laughter, and then I began to cry and words suddenly appeared in the sobs like fishes in streaming water: "Now the wheel moves . . . now the sand falls . . . now the nightbird shrieks . . . now it huddles together . . . now the tree crashes . . . now the viper quivers . . . now the wheel stops . . . now the Holy Books rise . . . now they are gone . . . now the wheel is still . . . now there is silence . . . now the leap is at hand . . . now the sands have run out . . . now the mountain roars . . . now the river gapes . . . now . . . now . . . they are here!" Then they beat my head with a stick until I fell down. Then they tied me to the ladder and raised it over the fire and the flames rushed at me and licked my clothes and before I fell face down on the blaze, I burned like a torch. Then they sang a hymn, *but I was no longer afraid.* He pressed His big body into mine and we fell into deep water . . . He locked me in His arms and I did not feel cold any more . . .

Long pause. Silence.

The Smith: Excuse me. I don't mean to bother you, but has anyone here seen my wife?

John: No, we haven't seen a soul . . . haven't seen as much as a cat.

The Smith: That's tough luck!

John: Did she get lost?

The Smith: She ran away . . . with a juggler.

John: If she has such bad taste, I think you ought to let her go, and not do her the honor of running around through the forest looking for her.

The Smith: I guess you're right, my boy . . . but I'm mad enough to kill her.

John: Well, now! That's another story!

The Smith: And if I ever lay my hands on *him* . . . I'm going to murder that cheap clown, too.

John: There are too many actors around anyway, so even if he hasn't done anything in particular, you ought to get rid of him.

The Smith: My wife has always been very much interested in the art of the theater.

John: And that was the cause of her downfall!

The Smith: Her downfall, not mine . . . you see, if a fellow is born at the bottom of the heap, he has no place to fall to. By the way, are you married?

John: Me? A hundred times and more! I can't even keep track of my wives, but that's the way it is when a man does a lot of traveling.

The Smith: One wife is worse than a hundred, let me tell you, or maybe I've just had worse luck than any other poor slob in this lousy world, but I wouldn't bet on it.

John: Yeah, it's hell with them and hell without them, so no matter how you figure it, it's all the same. I guess it makes sense to kill them while the fun is going on.

The Smith: Some fun! Your wife gabbing, your brats squawking, stinking diapers, spitefulness and scratches, slaps and pinches, and the Devil's dame for a mother-in-law. And when you fall into bed after a hard day and you're just about to doze off, then there's a new tune: weeping, wailing, and whining to high heaven.

Whines.

Why don't you kiss me goodnight?

John (same tone): Why don't you sing me a song?

The Smith: Why don't you notice my new drawers?

John: Why don't you make love to me the way you did when we first met?

The Smith: Why do you turn your back to me and snore?

John: Oh, me!

The Smith: Oh, my!

Suddenly angry.

Then along came that juggler, swinging down the lane, sighing and crying and strumming his damned lute. He had blue eyes and rosy cheeks and went in and out of my house with his tail in the air like a cat in heat. He stank of some sweet-smellin' stuff and was as full of soft-soap as you're full of guts. My mother-in-law was his lookout, while I got double-crossed so big you could have put me on the altar in the church.

John: And then they took off!

The Smith: I'll nip them with my pinchers. I'll smash them with my hammer. I'll ram my poker in their bellies!

He suddenly bursts into tears.

John: What in the name of all the saints in—! What are you bawling for?

The Smith: Yes, look at the blacksmith moaning and groaning like a baby with a diaperful.

John: It beat me! After all, you got rid of a double-dyed daughter of a dog!

The Smith: You just don't understand!

John: Oh, you mean your pride is hurt!

The Smith: No, I could stand that, all right.

John: And you call yourself a man? Like hell you are!

The Smith: Maybe I love her.

John: That's it! Maybe you *love* her! Don't you know that love is nothing but an itch in the groin that keeps itching and itching and is covered up with a damned lot of lies, deceptions, alibis, and general trickery? Love is the blackest of plagues, but unfortunately we don't die of it. If we did, there would at least be some release from the damned thing. Every once in a while you hear of an utter idiot who has died for love, but it's usually love that dies first . . .

it just fades away and dies. Love is a minor infectious disease like colds; it thins your blood, saps your strength, weakens your independence, and your morals—if you have any—begins to leave a bad taste in your mouth, and ends up with a yawn. The most perfect thing in this imperfect world is love, for love is perfect in its imperfection!

The Smith: You're lucky you have such a gift of gab. You've got yourself drunk on your own moonshine.

John: My dear sir, I'd like you to know that I've heard, read, and actually lived through most of the fairy tales about right and wrong that people are always telling each other. Yes, and all those childish fables in the Bible, about angels and holy spirits and such, leave me stone cold.

The Smith: Watch out! The night is coming on and the forest is dark. Watch what you're saying!

John (brags): This is my gospel: My little tummy is the world, my head is eternity, and my hands are two glorious suns. My legs are the unblest pendulums of time and my dirty feet are two magnificent starting points for my philosophy. I am the universe all by myself, nobody believes in it but me . . . everyone thinks it's ridiculous, sometimes I think so, too. Insignificant to heaven and indifferent to hell, altogether it's worth just about as much as a sneeze, the only difference being that a sneeze is more enjoyable.

The Smith: Oh God, now it's coming over me again!

John: What's bothering you?

The Smith: I just happened to think of my wife! She's so beautiful . . . so beautiful, you can't talk about her without soft music!

John: That's exactly what the juggler did with his little stringed instrument.

The Smith: Her eyes are like blueberries, her lips are like brandy, her breasts are like heavenly cucumbers, her behind like a juicy pear —all in all, she's as tempting as a patch of wild strawberries.

John: Wait a minute! You're a pretty lousy poet! You sound more like a peasant inspired by a vegetable garden.

The Knight (from a distance): Come, we must move on!

The Smith: I'd like to go along with you for a way, if it's all right.

John: It'st all right, if you don't start whining again. If you do, I'll leave you flat! Witch, are you ready? We're a motley crew, if ever I saw one!

They walk on. Music.

The Smith: Now the moon is rising.

John: It will be easier to see the road.

The Witch: I don't like the moon.

The music ends.

The Smith: The trees are so still tonight . . .

John: Because there is no wind.

The Smith: I mean, they're absolutely motionless.

John: Oooh! What was that?

The Witch: Those are the bats that have been flying across the road, past our faces.

The Smith: It's so deathly quiet, I wish at least I heard a fox.

John: Or an owl.

The Smith: Or a dog barking.

John: Or a human voice, apart from my own.

The Witch: The moonlight burns my eyes so that I can hardly see.

John: It's dangerous to stand still in the moonlight. Don't you know that!

They walk on in silence.

Maria: Can anyone tell me how to get to the border? This looks like a cattle path, so I suppose I've lost my way.

John: If you come along with us, you'll run into the plague . . . and if you go in the opposite direction, you'll also run into the plague . . . perhaps it will strike you right here and save you the trouble of going anywhere.

Maria: It's the plague I'm so terribly afraid of. I took my little boy out of the cradle and I've walked all day without meeting a soul. Would any of you happen to have a little bit of bread?

John: Here's a piece of crust. It's all I've got. If you can make a dent in it, you're better than I am. But, then, I have only two teeth.

Maria: Oh, thank you!

The Smith: Now give me strength . . . for the moment is at hand! Who is that peeping out from behind those trees if it isn't my Most Honorable Spouse . . . with juggler attached! I say there, won't you please come forward, my dear lady and my dear sir, for here and now justice shall be done! Good evening, my dear wife, I see that you are out for a little stroll with your lap dog, or whatever that is paddling along at your side.

The Actor: You filthy boor! How dare you insult this beloved lady, the most beautiful of all Helens!

The Smith: Her name is Lisa.

John: Mad Lisa . . . bad Lisa . . .

The Smith: Slut!

John: Graceless . . . Faithless . . .

The Smith: Butt!

John: An angel in the muck . . . you can finish it yourself . . .

The Smith: You gilded little chamberpot!

The Actor: You miserable short-haired bastard . . . your voice is cracked, your breath stinks, and you're musclebound! If I were in your lousy rags, I'd be so ashamed of myself, I'd go jump in the lake.

The Smith: I'll smash your jaw so you won't be able to do your monkey-tricks for the cannibals who come to see you.

The Actor: I'll kick you in the belly so hard your guts'll fly out of your ears.

Lisa: Oh, look at me, please! Look at me . . . a wretched, desperate woman! And listen to these men! That actor . . . just listen to his voice!

The Actor: My voice? My voice, of course! My organ!

Lisa: Yes, you have an organ. You even have a couple of bunions, but that doesn't make you a man, not by a long shot.

John: He's an actor, that's all. So why don't we cut out the conversation and just cut his throat?

Lisa: Please let me explain. When he came whispering his love-talk in my ear, I didn't know it was part of his repertory. When he took me in his arms for the first time, I had no idea that he had rehearsed that scene in front of a mirror and played it at an audition for a director. When his beard tickled me so nicely, I didn't know it was a fake; or that his bright smile was just a collection of false teeth—and rotten ones at that. He stole his perfumes, swiped his songs, and lifted all his little movements from other clowns. I'm beginning to wonder if he's really a human being like everyone else.

The Actor: If you think I'm going to apologize for being alive, you're mistaken . . . even though I'm an actor without a part, a doll without a doll's house, a poet without a rhyme, a lover without a lady friend . . . and all the fleas flee me. Well, my good man, I throw down my little toy sword! I don't intend to defend myself!

The Smith: You'd better get ready to fight and give me a chance to kill you. The least you can do is make me as mad as I was a minute ago.

The Actor (throws himself on the ground): All right, I'll put my dagger right here over my heart, and all you have to is is drive it in. One smart blow and a living example of unreality will be immediately transformed into a real live corpse.

Lisa (to the Smith): Well, do something! Don't just stand there with your mouth open! He's a disgrace to you and to himself. Put an end to the wretch! He's begging for it.

Pause.

If you haven't got the nerve, I'll do it myself!

The Actor: Oh, help!

Pause.

I'm dying.

Closes his eyes; goes limp.

The Smith: And that sweet thing is my wife!

Lisa: Come on, let's go. There's no use talking.

John: Yes, let's break it up. I don't feel so good.

The Smith: Something you ate is bothering you.

John: What's bothering me is that I had nothing to eat.

They walk on.

The Actor: Are they gone now? Yes, they've gone. Then I can get up. Where's my dagger? There! I almost feel ashamed that the dagger is only a "prop," and I definitely feel ashamed that I'm not really dead. Still it's flattering that they believed in my death. So I stand here feeling ashamed and flattered, although my audience has long since disappeared in the woods. I find it nauseating to stand here ashamed and flattered; on the other hand, there's a certain satisfaction in feeling nauseated at being ashamed and flattered. I suppose it's presumptuous to feel satisfaction because one is nauseated at standing here ashamed and flattered; but if I start thinking of my pride it gives me a headache and it suddenly seems foolish to stand here in the middle of a dark forest completely alone with a headache because I happen to suffer from pride at feeling satisfaction on account of the fact that I am nauseated at being ashamed and flattered. Help! Who's that sneaking up behind me? Who are you?

The Girl: I've come to take you to a dark and exacting master. He says he needs your lute. You will have to play at a dance tonight down at the stone near the border.

The Actor: I have no time.

The Girl: The severe master knew you would answer that way. He says you are lying.

The Actor: I have my performance—

The Girl: It's been canceled.

The Actor: My contract—

The Girl: Terminated.

The Actor: My children, my family . . .

The Girl: They manage better without you.

The Actor: Is there no way I can get out of it?

The Girl: No.

The Actor: No exceptions, no loopholes?

The Girl: No, there are no loopholes.

The Actor: He *must* be a severe master.

The Girl: He *is* a severe master.

The Actor: All right then, come on, let's go and try to find him before he gets angry.

The Girl: Why are you sighing?

The Actor: I'm just sighing. Is that forbidden?

Wind. Music.

Narrator: The wanderers are very tired. They have come to a forest glade where they lie down in the moss. Quietly they lie there and listen to their own quiet breathing, the measured beat of their pulses, and the wind moving quietly in the tops of the trees. Maria has withdrawn from the others with her child, and she gazes at the moonlight which is no longer still and dead but shimmering and mysterious.

Maria: One morning the Holy Maiden went down to the well to fetch water. Little lizards were gliding over the stones—sometimes in sunlight, sometimes in shadow. She leaned over the edge of the well and looked down into the dark water-mirror. Her cheeks had grown pale and hollow, her eyes large and glowing. It was hard to carry the Child that particular morning because of the white-hot sun. And that is why she cried a little and her tears fell into the water of the well. But soon she stopped and she felt better, almost happy, as she filled her pitcher. The sun flashed in the cold water, and it splashed over her red skirt and her bare feet. She washed away the salt of her tears that burned on her cheeks and took a drink of the fresh, sweet water. She drank out of her cupped hands as out of a bowl. Then the Child stirred in her womb, and she laughed aloud in her loneliness. She drew herself up, her arms pressed against her sides, and lifted the water jug in her strong brown hands. Then she climbed the few steps uphill to the house of the carpenter, moving through the glittering heat of the morning sunlight on feet that seemed to dance. A long way off she heard the sheep dogs barking and the cries of the shepherds as they drove their herds toward the mountains, toward the cool shade of the olive groves.

Pause.

And that's the story of the Maiden Maria.

John: But can anyone tell where we actually are?

Karin: You have reached the starting point, the stone at the border. You have walked in a circle and here you stand, in the wee hours of the morning, shivering and waiting. The wind has risen and the clouds gather on the horizon that is turning gray in the light of the dawn.

The Knight: Who are you?

Karin: I am the wife of the knight, Antonius Block. I left the castle because of the plague . . . One of the last to go . . . Don't you recognize me?

The Knight: And what are you doing here?

Karin: Do you see the fires over there? Do you hear the music? That's the neighboring country whose soldiers have blocked up the border with a high fence that runs from coast to coast. Everywhere there are soldiers, so that no one from our plague-stricken land can possibly get through. We must wait.

The Knight: Wait for what?

Karin: For nothing. For the plague. Poor Antonius Block, poor dear, you don't recognize me, do you? But I recognize you. Somewhere in your face, in your eyes—frightened and hidden—is the boy who left so many years ago. Was it worthwhile and exciting—the Crusade? Did you kill many pagans, ride like a demon, break swords and lances? Did you say many prayers at the Holy Grave, and rape many women . . . ?

The Knight: Oh, I'm so tired.

Karin: Do you feel cold? Would you like to have my shawl? No.

John (sings): In the sea the fishes play,
And stately ships go on their way—

He yawns noisily.

Karin: Hush! Don't you hear?

John: Hear what?

Karin: Now the cocks are crowing in the other country where the dawn lights the plain. Now the fires are going out. Now the wind is dying down. Now the rain is beginning to fall very quietly and gently. Now we stand here close together waiting for someone to come from over there. He is a mighty man, a knight, a gentleman . . . and by his side are a young girl and a juggler with his lute slung over his shoulder. And now they are coming this way, walking toward us through the silence of the rain-laden dawn.

Long pause.

John: Good morning, Milord. We stand here huddled together waiting for you. My name is John, plain John, who walks and talks incessantly. And moping over there is a skinny and miserable knight with a lot of feverish and rambling thoughts under his hat.

Karin: I am the wife of the knight. And there stands a little witch who had an affair with the Black Fiend—or so the story goes. She had to burn for her sin, and I suppose she feels pretty low right now.

The Smith: I'm a blacksmith by trade, and a pretty good one at that, if I do say so myself. And that one, over there, is my wife Lisa —curtsy for the gentleman, Lisa. She's pretty hard to deal with sometimes, and we've just had a little spat, so to speak, but no worse than most other people.

Lisa: It was all that juggler's fault. You can ask him yourself— he's standing right there.

The Smith: Shut up, Lisa. There's a lady over there who calls herself Maria. She's been running day and night from the plague, and not so much for her own sake as for the child's. But now she's sitting there very quietly . . . waiting.

The Knight: Stern Master, will you listen to me! Every morning and evening I reach out towards heaven, towards God. I call on the Saints, I fill their ears with my cries, and again and again my heart overflows with faith. Across a spiritual desert, I feel God's nearness like the vibrations of a mighty bell. Suddenly my emptiness is filled with music of no tone, as if in waves of innumerable voices. In the great darkness I cry out, and my cry is like a whimper. For your glory, oh God! I live for your glory! For your glory! So I call out in the dark. Then a terrible thing happens in every fiber of my body . . . the flame of my faith dies suddenly as if someone had blown it out. The great bell falls silent, the darkness throbs and thickens, it presses against my mouth and forces itself down my throat. Then the curses explode out of my belly, out of my eyes, out of my hair, like the roars of wild beasts, the hisses of poisonous snakes, the hoarse shrieks of evil birds . . . and the darkness is splattered with blood . . . and my old wounds run with pus.

John: With all due respect for this Grave Gentleman, I wish you

would stop squawking. You say, you live out there in the darkness
—well, we all live right here like silly little specks of dust floating
in space—and in that darkness you find that there is no one who
listens to your complaints or is moved by your sufferings. Well, wash
away your tears and let your face reflect your indifference. I could
have given you some herbs to clean out your troubles with eternity,
but I suppose it's too late now. Anyway, in your very last minutes,
you will feel a terrific triumph at being able to roll your eyes and
wiggle your toes.

Karin: Quiet, quiet!

John: All right, I'll be quiet—but under protest. It's true, a
minute ago I was a little shy. But, if I've got to give up the ghost,
it won't be of my own free will and without a fight—with all due
respect, of course, for the Grave Gentleman.

Karin: Hush, hush! The actor is tuning up his lute. The Grave
Gentleman bids us dance. He wants us to take each other's hands
and form a chain. He himself will lead us, and the actor will bring
up the rear. Away from the dawn we shall go with measured tread,
away to the dark lands while the rain caresses our faces.

Whispers.

Arrange yourselves for the dance, my friends, my children. The
Grave Gentleman quickly loses his patience and the music has
just . . .

She is silent. The music of the lute. All move in a solemn dance.

CURTAIN.

Filmography

For complete cast and production credits, consult the film index in Jörn Donner's *The Personal Vision of Ingmar Bergman* (Bloomington: Indiana University Press, 1964) and the filmography in Robin Wood's *Ingmar Bergman* (New York: Frederick A. Praeger, Inc., 1970). Both sources also list a bibliography of Bergman's printed work.

FILMS

Torment (Hets), Svensk Filmindustri. 1944. Director: Alf Sjöberg.

Crisis (Kris), Svensk Filmindustri. 1946. Script: Leck Fischer, Ingmar Bergman.

It Rains on Our Love (Det regnar på vår kärlek), Lorens Marmstedt for Sveriges Folkbiografer. 1946. Script: Oscar Braathen, Herbert Grevenius, Ingmar Bergman.

Woman without a Face (Kvinna utan ansikte), Svensk Filmindustri. 1947. Director: Gustaf Molander.

A Ship to India (Skepp till Indialand), Lorens Marmstedt for Sveriges Folkbiografer, 1947. Script: Martin Söderhjelm, Ingmar Bergman.

Night Is My Future (Musik i mörker), Lorens Marmstedt/Terrafilm. 1947. Script: Dagmar Edqvist.

Port of Call (Hamnstad), Svensk Filmindustri. 1948. Script: Olle Länsberg, Ingmar Bergman.

Eva, Svensk Filmindustri. 1948. Script: Ingmar Bergman, Gustaf Molander. Director: Gustaf Molander.

The Devil's Wanton (Fängelse, Prison), Lorens Marmstedt/Terrafilm. 1949.

Three Strange Loves (Törst, Thirst), Svensk Filmindustri. 1949. Script: Birgit Tengroth, Herbert Grevenius.

Except where indicated otherwise, Ingmar Bergman is both script-writer and director of films listed in the filmography. English title in parentheses refers to name of film when released in Britain.

To Joy (Till glädje), Svensk Filmindustri, 1950.

While the City Sleeps (Medan staden sover), Svensk Filmindustri. 1950. Script: Lars-Eric Kjellgren, P. A. Fogelström, Ingmar Bergman. Director: Lars-Eric Kjellgren.

This Can't Happen Here (Sånt händer inte här), Svensk Filmindustri. 1950. Script: Herbert Grevenius.

Illicit Interlude (Sommarlek), Svensk Filmindustri. 1951. Script: Ingmar Bergman, Herbert Grevenius.

Divorced (Frånskild), Svensk Filmindustri. 1951. Script: Ingmar Bergman, Herbert Grevenius. Director: Gustaf Molander.

Secrets of Women (Kvinnors väntan), Svensk Filmindustri, 1952.

Monika (Sommaren med Monika), Svensk Filmindustri. 1953. Script: P. A. Fogelström, Ingmar Bergman.

The Naked Night (Gycklarnas afton, Sawdust and Tinsel), Sandrews. 1953.

A Lesson in Love (En lektion i kärlek), Svensk Filmindustri. 1954.

Dreams (Kvinnodröm), Sandrews. 1955.

Smiles of a Summer Night (Sommarnattens leende), Svensk Filmindustri. 1955.

The Last Couple Out (Sista paret ut), Svensk Filmindustri, 1956. Script: Ingmar Bergman, Alf Sjöberg. Director: Alf Sjöberg.

The Seventh Seal (Det sjunde inseglet), Svensk Filmindustri. 1957.

Wild Strawberries (Smultronstället), Svensk Filmindustri. 1957.

Brink of Life (Nära livet), Nordisk Tonefilm. 1957. Script: Ulla Isaksson.

The Magician (Ansiktet, The Face), Svensk Filmindustri. 1958.

The Virgin Spring (Jungfrukällan), Svensk Filmindustri. 1960. Script: Ulla Isaksson.

The Devil's Eye (Djävulens öga), Svensk Filmindustri. 1960.

Through a Glass Darkly (Såsom i en spegel), Svensk Filmindustri. 1961.

Lustgården, Svensk Filmindustri. 1961. Script: "Buntel Eriksson" (Ingmar Bergman, Erland Josephson). Director: Alf Kjellin.

Winter Light (Nattvardsgästerna, The Communicants), Svensk Filmindustri. 1962.

The Silence (Tystnaden), Svensk Filmindustri. 1963.

Not to Speak about All These Women (För att inte tala om alla dessa kvinnor), Svensk Filmindustri. 1964. Script: Ingmar Bergman, Erland Josephson.

Stimulantia, Svensk Filmindustri. 1966. Series of episodes directed by a number of Swedish directors. Ingmar Bergman's episode entitled *Daniel*.

Persona, Svensk Filmindustri. 1966.

Hour of the Wolf (Vargtimmen), Svensk Filmindustri. 1966. (Premiere 1968).

Shame (Skammen), Svensk Filmindustri. 1967.
Passion of Anna (En passion), Svensk Filmindustri. 1969.
The Touch (Beröringen), Svensk Filmindustri. 1970.
Whisperings and Cries (Viskningar och rop), Cinematograph & Swedish Film Institute. 1972.

TV FILMS

The Ritual (Riten), Cinematograph. 1968.
Fårö, Cinematograph. 1970.
Reservatet, Cinematograph, 1971.

Selected Bibliography

The most complete listing of writings by and about Ingmar Bergman may be found in the following studies:

Cowie, Peter. *Sweden 2*. New York: A. S. Barnes & Co., 1970. Pp. 251–56.
Donner, Jörn. *The Personal Vision of Ingmar Bergman*. Bloomington: Indiana University Press, 1964. Pp. 255–65.
Steene, Birgitta. *Ingmar Bergman*. New York: Twayne Publishers, Inc., 1968. Pp. 149–54.

I. INGMAR BERGMAN: BOOKS

Béranger, Jean. *Ingmar Bergman et ses films*. Paris: Le Terrain Vague, 1959. (Revised edition, 1960).
Björkman, Stig; Manns, Torsten; & Sima, Jonas. *Bergman om Bergman*. Stockholm: Norstedt & Söner, 1970. English translation by Paul Britten Austin to be published by Simon & Schuster, New York.
Burvenich, Jos. *Thèmes d'inspiration d'Ingmar Bergman*. Brussels: Club du livre de cinéma, 1960.
* Carril, Martinez M. *Ingmars ansikte*. Montevideo: Cuadernos de Cine Club del Uruguay, 1964.
Chiaretti, Tommaso. *Ingmar Bergman*. Rome: Canesi, 1964.
Cowie, Peter. *Antonioni, Bergman, Resnais*. London: Tantivy Press, 1963.
*———. *Sweden 2*. London: A. Zwemmer Ltd.; New York: A. S. Barnes & Co., 1970. Pp. 95–197.
Cuenca, Carlos Fernandez. *Introduccion al estudio de Ingmar Bergman*. Madrid: Filmoteca de Espana, 1961.
Donner, Jörn. *Djävulens ansikte: Ingmar Bergmans filmer*. Stockholm: Bokförlaget Aldus-Bonniers, 1962. (2nd edition 1965.) English translation: *The Personal Vision of Ingmar Bergman*. Translated by Holger Lundbergh. Bloomington: Indiana University Press, 1964.
Gibson, A. *The Silence of God*. New York: Harper & Row, Inc., 1969.

* Items marked with an asterisk are included or represented in the text of this volume.

* Höök, Marianne. *Ingmar Bergman*. Stockholm: Wahlström & Widstrand, 1962.

Siclier, Jacques. *Ingmar Bergman*. Editions Universitaires, 8. Paris: Classiques du Cinéma, 1960.

* Steene, Birgitta. *Ingmar Bergman*. New York: Twayne Publishers, Inc., 1968.

Thevenet, H. Alsina, and Monegal, Emir Rodriguez. *Ingmar Bergman, un dramaturgo cinematografico*. Montevideo: Ediciones Renacimiento, 1964.

Wood, Robin. *Ingmar Bergman*. New York: Frederick A. Praeger, Inc., 1969.

II. INGMAR BERGMAN: PUBLISHED SCREENPLAYS

En filmtrilogi (Såsom i en spegel, Nattvardsgästerna, Tystnaden). Stockholm: Norstedt, 1963.

Persona. Stockholm: Norstedt, 1963.

Four Screenplays of Ingmar Bergman (Smiles of a Summer Night, The Seventh Seal, Wild Strawberries, The Magician). Translated by Lars Malmström and David Kushner. New York: Simon Schuster, 1960; London: Secker and Warburg, 1960.

A Trilogy (Through a Glass Darkly, Winter Light, The Silence). Translated by Paul Britten Austin. London: Calder & Boyars, 1967.

Ingmar Bergman. Oeuvres (Sommarlek, La nuit des forains, Sourires d'une nuit d'été, Le septième sceau, Les fraises sauvages, Le visage). Translated by C. G. Bjurström and Maurice Pons. Paris: Robert Laffont, 1962.

III. ARTICLES AND REVIEWS ON *The Seventh Seal* [1]

Allombert, Guy. "Le septième sceau." *Document Image et Son,* no. 119 (February 1959):I–VIII.

Archer, Eugene. "The Rack of Life." *Film Quarterly* 12, no. 4 (Summer 1959):3–16. An appreciative discussion of Bergman's production up to 1958.

Björkman, C. "Mörk Bergmanfilm med ljuspunkter." *Dagens Nyheter,* February 17, 1957.

Blackwood, Caroline. "The Mystique of Ingmar Bergman." *Encounter* 16, no. 91 (April 1961):54–57. Very critical of Bergman's "Nordic gloom." Includes a brief discussion of *The Seventh Seal*.

Cowie, Peter. "Great Films of the Century: *The Seventh Seal*." *Films and*

---

[1] Including some articles surveying Bergman's work in the 1950s.

Filming, 9, no. 1 (January 1963):25–29. Gives excellent resumé of film's reception in England.

Croce, Arlene. "The Bergman Legend." *Commonweal* 71, no. 24 (March 11, 1960):647–49. Places Bergman in his native cinematic tradition. Calls him an "erratic" filmmaker but a true *directeur de conscience.*

* Crowther, Bosley. *The Great Films: Fifty Golden Years of Motion Pictures.* New York: G. P. Putnam's Sons, 1967. Pp. 218–22.

Dixon, Campbell. "Dance Macabre." *The Daily Telegraph,* March 8, 1958.

Dienstfrey, Harris. "The Success of Ingmar Bergman." *Commentary* 32, no. 5 (November 1961):391–98. Critical survey of Bergman's films of the 1950s. Finds Bergman's vision "arbitrary" and "unreal," and his camera work "magic" but "beautifying."

* Dyer, John Peter. *"The Seventh Seal." Sight and Sound* 27, no. 4 (Spring 1958):199–200.

* Fovez, Elie, Ayfre, Amédée, and d'Yvoire, Jean. *"Le septième sceau." Télé-ciné* no. 77 (August–September 1958), Fiche 333.

* Fürstenau, Theo. "Apocalypse und Totentantz." *Die Zeit,* February 16, 1962.

* H.H. *"The Seventh Seal." Films in Review* 11 (November 1958):515–17.

* Harrie, Ivar. "Ingmar Bergman vill vara sveriges Kaj Munk." *Expressen,* March 2, 1957.

* Hibbin, Nina. "Y Certificate." *The Daily Worker,* March 8, 1958.

* Hjertén, Hanserik. *"Det sjunde inseglet." Dagstidningen,* February 17, 1957.

Holland, Norman. *"The Seventh Seal:* The Film as Iconography." *The Hudson Review* 12, no. 2 (Summer 1959):266–70. Mostly a review but contains a discussion of the chess game in *The Seventh Seal.*

Hood, Robin. *"Det sjunde inseglet." Stockholms-Tidningen,* February 17, 1958.

Jarvie, Ian. "Notes on the Films of Ingmar Bergman." *Film Journal* (Melbourne) 14 (November 1959):9–17. Survey of Bergman's films of the 1950s. Very critical of *The Seventh Seal* for its lack of intellectual clarity.

Landkvist, John. "Så stora smultron finns inte. . . ." *Aftonbladet,* February 25, 1957.

Lejeune, C. A. "Dance Macabre." *The Observer,* March 9, 1958.

* Löthwall, Lars-Olof. "Ingmar Bergman och Digerdöden." *Stockholms-Tidningen,* July 5, 1956.

* Mambrino, Jean. "Traduit du silence." *Cahiers du Cinéma* 14, no. 83 (May 1958):43–46.

Napolitano, Antonio. *"Dal settimo sigillo alle soglie della vita." Cinema nuovo,* no. 151 (May–June 1961):69–75. Very abstract discussion of Bergman's films from *The Seventh Seal* to *Brink of Life.*

* Powell, Dilys. "Wormwood for You and Me." *The Sunday Times,* March 9, 1958.

Quigly, Isabel. "Cardboard Pastoral." *The Spectator* 200, no. 6768 (March 14, 1958):326.

* Roemer, Michael. "Views and Reviews: Bergman's Bag of Tricks." *The Reporter* 26, no. 4 (February 15, 1962):37–42.

* Rohmer, Eric. "Avec Le septième sceau Bergman nous offre son Faust." *Arts,* April 23–29, 1958.

Roos, Hans-Dieter. "Keine Antwort auf die Frage nach Gott." *Süddeutsche Zeitung,* April 26, 1962. *The Seventh Seal* was not shown in West Germany until 1962, in the aftermath of such successes as *Wild Strawberries* and *Through a Glass Darkly.*

* Sarris, Andrew. *"The Seventh Seal." Film Culture* 19 (1959):51–61.

* Schein, Harry. "Poeten Bergman." *BLM* 26, no. 4 (April 1957):350–53.

* Schildt, Jurgen. "Spelet om godheten och döden." *Vecko-Journalen,* no. 9 (1957).

* Scott, James F. "The Achievement of Ingmar Bergman." *Journal of Aesthetics and Arts,* 24, no. 2 (Winter 1965):263–72.

Simon, John. "Ingmar, the Image-Maker." *The Mid-Century,* no. 29 (December 1960):9–12. A discussion of Bergman's visual talent in connection with the Mid-Century Book Club selection of *Four Screenplays of Ingmar Bergman.*

Time, March 14, 1960. Cover story on Ingmar Bergman.

Whitebait, William. "Death and the Knight." *The New Statesman* 55, no. 1408 (March 8, 1958):303.

* Young, Colin. *"The Seventh Seal." Film Quarterly* 12, no. 3 (Spring 1959):42–44.

Index